The Little Black Princess

Princess

A True Story from the Never-Never

JEANNIE GUNN

ETT IMPRINT

Exile Bay

This edition published by ETT Imprint, Exile Bay 2021

First published 1905.

ETT IMPRINT
PO Box R1906

Royal Exchange NSW 1225
Australia

ISBN 978-1-922473-49-3 (paper)
ISBN 978-1-922473-50-9 (ebook)

Cover and internal design by Tom Thompson

CONTENTS

'Bett-Bett' - Dolly Bonson, who died aged 95 in 1988.

1

Bett-Bett

Bett-Bett must have been a Princess, for she was a King's niece, and if that does not make a Princess of any one, it ought to do so!

She didn't sit—like fairy-book princesses—waving golden sceptres over devoted subjects, for she was just a little bush girl or 'lubra,' about eight years old. She had, however, a very wonderful palace—the great lonely Australian bush.

She had also: one devoted subject—a little speckled dog called Sue; one big trouble—looking out tucker'; and one big fear—Debbil-debbils!

It wasn't all fun being a black Princess, for nobody knew what terrible things might happen any minute—as you will see!

Once, when Bett-Bett and Sue were camped with some of the tribe on the Roper River, they were suddenly attacked by the Willeroo blacks, who were their very fiercest enemies. Everybody 'ran bush' at once to hide, with the Willeroos full chase after them. In the fright and hurry-scurry Bett-Bett fell into the river, and at once decided to stay there, for in spite of crocodiles it was the safest place she could think of. She swam under the water to the steep banks, and caught hold of the roots of an old tree. Standing on this, she stuck her nose and mouth out of the water, in the shelter of a water-lily leaf, and there she stood for a long, long time without moving a muscle, her little naked black body looking exactly like one of the shadows.

When all was quiet and it was getting dark, she crept out,

thinking she would be safe for the night. Sue at once came out from her hiding-place, and licking Bett-Bett's hand, seemed to say:

'My word, that was a narrow escape, wasn't it!'

Bett-Bett spoke softly to her, and the two of them then hunted about to see if any "tucker" had been left behind.

Sue very soon found a piece of raw beef, and Bett-Bett made a fire in the scrub, so that nobody could see the smoke; then, while the supper was cooking, they crouched close to the warmth, for they felt very cold. By and by the steak caught fire, and Bett-Bett picked it up between two sticks, and tried to blow it out. Finding she could not manage this, she laid it on the ground and threw a handful of earth on it, and at once the flames died away. She and Sue then grinned at each other as if to say, 'Aren't we clever? we know how to manage things, don't we?' and were just settling down to enjoy their supper, when a dreadful thing happened—somebody grabbed Bett-Bett from behind and shouted out,'Hallo! what name you?"

Did you ever see a terribly frightened little black princess? I did, for I saw one then. I was 'the Missus" from the homestead, and with the Boss, or 'Maluka' (as the blacks always called him), was 'out bush', camping near the river. We had arrived just about sunset, and seeing black tracks had decided to follow them, and found Bett-Bett! Big Mac, one of the stockmen, was with us, and it was he who had caught hold of her, but if it had been an army of Debbil-debbils she could not have been more frightened.

'Nang ah! piccaninny,'I said, meaning 'come here, little one.' I spoke as kindly as I could, and Bett-Bett saw at once that I was a friend.

She spoke to Sue and came, saying: 'Me plenty savey Engliss, Missus!" This surprised us all, for she looked such a wild little girl. I asked her where she had learnt her "plenty savey Engliss',' and she answered, 'Longa you boys,' meaning she had picked it up from our homestead boys.

After a little coaxing she told us the story of the Willeroos, and said 'Dank you please, Missus', very earnestly when I asked if she would like to sleep in our camp.

As we went up the bank I was amused to see that she was munching her beef. It takes more than a good fright to make a blackfellow let go his only chance of supper. After a big meal of 'damper' and honey—sugar-bag' she called it—she went to a puddle and smeared herself all over with mud, and when I asked why she did this she said: ''S'pose skeeto come on, him bite mud, him no more bite me meself,'and I thought her a very wise little person.

As soon as it became dark, she and Sue curled themselves up into a little heap near the fire, and fell asleep for the night.

In the morning I gave her a blue and white singlet that I had taken from one of the boys 'swags'. She dressed herself in it at once, and looked just like a gaily-coloured beetle, with thin black arms and legs, but she thought herself very stylish, and danced about everywhere with Sue at her heels. All Aboriginal dogs are ugly, but Sue was the ugliest of them all. She looked very much like a flattened out plum-pudding on legs, with ears like a young calf, and a cat's tail!

As we sat at breakfast I asked Bett-Bett if any mosquitoes had bitten her in the night, 'No more,' she said, and then added with a grin: 'Big mob bin sing out, sing out.' She seemed pleased to think how angry they must have been when they found a mouthful of mud, instead of the juicy girl they expected.

When we were ready to start for the homestead I asked Bett-Bett if she and Sue would like to come and live with me there. 'Dank you please, Missus!' she answered, grinning with delight.

So Bett-Bett found a Missus, and I — well, I found a real nuisance!!

2

'Shimmy Shirts'

FOR at least a week after we reached the homestead, Bett-Bett was kept busy protecting Sue from the station dogs. We hadn't been home an hour before we heard a fearful yell, and running to see what could have happened, found that all the dogs on the place had set on the poor little beast, and were trying to worry her to death.

With a shriek Bett-Bett flew to the rescue. As she ran she picked up a thick stick, and with it fought and hammered and screamed her way into the biting, yelping mob of dogs; then picking up the dusty little speckled ball, she fought and hammered and screamed her way out again to a place of safety. There she sat and crooned over Sue, who licked her face and tried to say—'How good you are, Bett-Bett.'

I don't know how many fights we had altogether, for the dogs kept at it till they were tired of the fun, which was not before Sue was nearly in tatters.

While Bett-Bett was fighting these battles I was busy sewing, making clothes for her. To begin with, I made her a bright blue dress which pleased her very much, and the singlet was kept for a night-dress, for she would not part with it altogether. Then I made some little white petticoats which she called 'Shimmy Shirts.' When these were finished I began to make a red dress; but oh dear, the fuss she made! and the fright she got into! In funny pidgin English and with much waving of her arms, she said that if you had on a red dress when there was a thunderstorm the Debbil-debbil who made the thunder would 'come on' and kill you 'dead-fellow'. When I heard

The homestead, Elsey Station, on the Roper River.

Bett-Bett and Sue, her dog - 'Me plenty savey Engliss, Missus'

this, of course I made a pink dress, as I didn't want the Thunder-Debbil-debbil to run off with her. Besides, he might have been angry with me for making red dresses for little native girls.

This Debbil-debbil is a funny sort of person, for although he gets furious if he sees a lubra dressed in red, it pleases him wonderfully to see an old blackfellow with as much red on as he can find. Do you know, if this Thunder-Debbil-debbil is roaring dreadfully, and happens to catch sight of an old man with plenty of red handkerchiefs, and scarves of red feathers tied round him, it puts him into such a good temper that he can't help smiling, and then nobody gets hurt. But sometimes even a blackfellow with yards of red stuff wound round him can do nothing to quiet this raging Debbil-debbil; then everybody knows that the lubras have been wearing red dresses. Such wicked, selfish people deserve to be punished, and it's quite a comfort to think that very soon Mr. Thunder-Debbil-debbil will get hold of them and 'kill them deadfellow'. Of course, if anybody gets killed by mistake, it will be their fault, for they should have given all their red things to their husbands.

Billy Muck, one of the wise old men of the tribe, told Bett-Bett this fearful story. Bett-Bett was engaged to be married to Billy Muck, and it was his duty to teach her these things. I fancy Billy made it up, I don't know; but the wise old men, who are supposed to know everything, have a cunning little way of telling awful tales about Debbil-debbils, so as to get the best things for themselves.

For ages upon ages the old men have told the young men and lubras that they must not eat fat turkeys, or the tail of the kangaroo, or indeed any of the best things that they find when hunting. If they do, a terrible thing will happen, for a big hunting Debbil-debbil will come on with a rush, and in a moment make them very old and weak. 'Look at us!' cry the old rascals. 'We eat these things, and behold, we are weak old men, with no strength to fight an enemy!' This looks so true that nobody — excepting the old men — cares about eating turkeys, and kangaroo tails, and such things.

Bett-Bett believed all these tales, for she was a little black, every bit of her. Like all blacks, she had such a generous heart that she could not bear to have anything good without sharing it with everybody. This was rather a nuisance, for as soon as her clothes were finished she wanted to give most of them to the other lubras.

'Him no more got goodfellow dress, Missus,' she said, almost crying, when I told her she must keep her clothes for herself. I didn't know what to do; it seemed wrong to teach her to be greedy and selfish, so I had to say that I would make the lubras a new dress each.

This made everybody shriek with delight and for another week we had a merry time choosing colours, sewing dresses, and conducting dog fights. Fortunately the lubras said that 'Shimmy Shirts' were 'silly fellow, or I suppose I would have had to make enough of these to go round as well.

Among the things I had given Bett-Bett was a warm 'bluey' or rug, and wrapped in this she and Sue slept on the bath-room floor every night. She preferred the floor to a bed, and was very funny about my spring Mattress — 'Him too muchee jump-up jump-up,' she said scornfully.

At bedtime, dressed in her gay singlet, she made her bed. First she spread her 'bluey' out on the floor, and jumped and pranced wildly about till she had managed to fold it in four, Then she lifted a corner carefully, and she and Sue crept in like a pair of young opossums. While they were settling themselves the rug bulged and wobbled and wriggled so much, that it looked as though it were playing at earthquakes. At last, when all was quiet, two pairs of very bright eyes peeped out at the top of the bluey, looking for the supper biscuit that I always had ready. As soon as I offered it, out came a thin black arm, and then Bett-Bett, Sue and biscuit disappeared for the night.

It was no use trying to keep these two apart. They simply could not understand why they should not sleep together; so I told Bett-Bett that Sue must have plenty of baths, and that if I ever found one single tick on her, the little dog would have to be given a whipping.

The thought of such a fearful punishment for them both made Bett-Bett shiver with fear. She called Sue and told her all about it, and made her understand that she would have to lie still and be hunted in, so that every horrid little insect could be found and killed. So every day, and many times a day, they had a tick-hunt, and Bett-Bett managed to make a great game of it.

She talked to herself all the time, and pretended that the ticks were wicked people, and that she was a terrible Debbil-debbil, who caught them and killed them 'dead-fellow'. How she did grin as she scrunched them between two stones.

One morning Bett-Bett was very quiet on the verandah, with Sue asleep beside her. I wondered what she was doing, and went out to see. She was busy unravelling threads from some pieces of rag, and I asked her what they were for. 'Me makem string,' she answered, and taking up a few threads, stuck one of her thin little legs straight out in front of her. Pulling up her dress, she laid the threads on her thigh, and with the palm of her hand rolled them quickly backwards and forwards. In a few seconds she grinned and held up a little piece of string in her fingers.

I was very interested, and sat watching her till she had made quite a yard; then, to help to amuse her, gave her a big bundle of coloured scraps of rag.

After a day or two, she came and showed me a pretty little bag that she had made, by weaving and knotting this string together.

'You are a good little girl, Bett-Bett,' I said. 'Now come and help me tidy your box.'

When her clean clothes were neatly in place, I found that the 'Shimmy Shirts' were all missing, and asked where they were.

'Me knock up longa Shimmy Shirts,' Bett-Bett said with a grin, meaning that she was tired of wearing them.

'But where are they?' I said.

'Longa string,' she answered cheerfully. 'Me bin make em.'

Then I knew that the piles of rag she had unravelled to make into string were her new 'Shimmy Shirts'.

I was really angry with her now, and set her to sew at a new one. She obeyed with such a cheerful grin that I began to feel quite mean for punishing her, for how could she understand that it was wrong to tear up her own things?

I was just going to tell her to run and play, when I heard a merry little chuckle from under the verandah. Looking to see what the fun was, I found that Bett-Bett was having a tick-hunt. She had just found an extra big one between Sue's toes, which she dragged from its hiding-place and threaded on to her needle and cotton. As she held her thread up for me to admire, I saw that she had about a dozen of the horrid creatures, hanging down like a string of beads. I felt quite sick.

'Bett-Bett,' I said, 'you have done enough sewing; take some soap, and go and give yourself and Sue a good bath.'

Off they went to the creek like a pair of gay young wallabies, hopping and skipping over everything.

In a few minutes they were both nearly white with soap lather, dancing a wild sort of corrobboree on an old tree trunk. The dance ended suddenly with a leap into 'middle water', as Bett-Bett called the deep holes.

They loved a bath, these two — 'bogey', the blacks call it — but neither of them would have soap on their faces.

'Him'— meaning the soap —'bite eye belonga me,' Bett-Bett explained.

Belts of red feathers . . . to please "Mr. Thunder Debbil-debbil."

Bett-Bett's "Shimy Shirt" bag.

Sticks for procuring fire by friction.

3

Shut-him-eye Quickfellow

THE King we were talking about — Bett-Bett's uncle, you know — was called by the tribe Ebimel Wooloomool. The white people had nicknamed him 'Goggle Eye', and he was very proud of his 'whitefellow name', as he called it. You see, he didn't know what it meant.

He didn't have a golden sceptre. Australian kings never do; but he had what was quite as deadly — a 'Magic Death-bone'. If you had been up to mischief, breaking the laws, or doing anything wrong, it was wise to keep out of his way; for every blackfellow knew that if he 'sang' this bone and pointed it at you, you would very quickly die.

The white man says you die of fright; but as it is the bone-pointing that gives the fright, it's the bone-pointing that kills, isn't it? But I'll tell you more about this by and bye.

The first time I met Goggle Eye, he was weeding my garden, and I didn't know he was a King; I thought he was just an ordinary blackfellow. You see he didn't have a crown, and as he was only wearing a tassel and a belt made from his mother-in-law's hair, it was no wonder I made the mistake. It takes a good deal of practice to tell a King at a glance — when he's naked and pulling up weeds.

I didn't like having even naked Kings about the homestead, so I said—

'Goggle Eye, don't you think you had better have some more clothes on?'

He grinned and looked very pleased, so I gave him a pair of blue cotton trousers. He put them on at once, without even troubling to go behind a bush, and asked my advice as to which leg he had better put in first. I gave him all the help I could and at last had him safely into them, right side out, and the front where it ought to be.

We gardened for a while, the old man and I, but as the sun became hotter I noticed that he kept pulling his trousers up over his knees. At last he sat down and took one leg right out.

'What's the matter, Goggle Eye?' I asked. 'Don't you like your Trousers"

'Him bite me longa knee,' he answered, meaning that they pinched him under the knee; then picking up his hoe again he worked till dinner time with one leg in and one out, and the trunk of the trousers fixed in some extraordinary way to his belt. After dinner he took both legs out and worked with the trousers dangling in front of him.

'Too muchee hot fellow,' he explained. Next morning he was dressed in his cool and airy tassel and belt, and nothing else.

'Where are your trousers, Goggle Eye?' I asked, and, 'Me bin knock up longa trousa,' was all he said.

A few days afterwards I met his lubra with a tucker-bag made of one of the legs; so I wasted no more trousers on his Majesty the King.

I was always ready to listen to any old blackfellow telling about the strange laws and customs of the tribe. Very soon Goggle Eye found this out, and as sitting in the shade, yarning, suited the old rascal much better than gardening, we had many a long gossip.

I never laughed at their strange beliefs. I found them wonderfully interesting, for I soon saw that under every silly little bit of nonsense was a great deal of good sense. At first it appears great nonsense to tell the young men that fat turkeys and kangaroo tails will make them old and weak; but it does not seem so silly when we know that it is only a blackfellow's way of providing for old age.

When Goggle Eye found that I never made fun of the laws that he thought so good and wise, he would tell me almost anything that I wanted to know. I was a particular friend of his, but he was not at all pleased with me for bringing Bett-Bett to the homestead; in fact, he was quite cross about it. He said he was her 'little bit father', and seemed to think that explained everything. By 'little bit father' he meant he was her father's brother, or cousin, or some near relation of his. I really could not see what difference it made, if he was her uncle, I just thought him a very disagreeable old man, and soon forgot all about it.

About a week after, Bett-Bett and I were gardening, and I sent her to the store-room for a hammer, so that I could fix up some creepers. While she was gone his Majesty the King came along, and I kept him to help me.

As Bett-Bett came back round the corner of the house, she saw him and shut her eyes at once, and of course the next minute bumped her head on one of the verandah posts.

'Open your eyes, you foolish child,' I called, for with them still tightly shut she was feeling her way into the house.

'Can't longa Goggle Eye,' she answered, and dropping the hammer on the ground, slipped through the doorway.

'Bring me the hammer, Goggle Eye,' I said, turning to him, only to find that his eyes were shut too.

'You silly old thing,' I said, 'playing baby-tricks', for I thought they were having a game of something like white children's 'saw you last'; 'bring me that hammer at once, I can't stand on this ladder all day.' But he would not move or open his eyes till I told him that Bett-Bett had gone away. When we had finished the creeper, I sent him to the creek for a bucket of water and called Bett-Bett to come and pull up weeds. She came, but as she worked kept one eye on the creek, and the minute that Goggle Eye's head appeared over the banks, walked towards the house.

'Bett-Bett,' I said sternly, 'stay here,' for I was tired of their silly games.

'Can't, Missus,' she answered, stopping but shutting her eyes. 'Goggle Eye little bit father belonga me.'

'I can't help that,' I said, losing all patience. 'Stay here, I want you both.'

She stayed, but old Goggle Eye stopped short. He called a lubra, who came and shrieked out something, and Bett-Bett crying: 'Must, Missus, straightfellow,' ran round the house to the far side.

'Whatever is the matter with you all?' I said, for I saw now they were not playing a game. 'Come here, Goggle Eye, and tell me what this all means. And, Bett-Bett, you stay where you are.'

His Majesty came, and sitting down under the verandah, began to tell of one of the strangest customs that the blacks have.

The wise men of the tribe, he explained, have always taught that you must never, never look at any little girl or lubra if you are her 'little-bit-father', or 'little-bit-brother', or any near relation to her. You must not even speak to her, or listen to her voice, unless she is so far off that you cannot see her face. 'That far— ' said Goggle Eye, pointing to a tree about one hundred yards away.

I was very interested and asked him what would happen if he broke this law. He answered earnestly: 'Spose me look, Debbil-debbil take away eye; spose me listen, Debbil-debbil take away ear; spose me talk, Debbil-debbil take away tongue.'

'Dear me,' I said, 'that would be unpleasant,' and then I asked him why the Debbil-debbils didn't come and catch him when he was talking to Maudie. She, I knew, was his sister, and he often spoke to her. He looked at me very scornfully, 'Him bin come on first time, me bin come on *bee*hind,' he said, meaning that she had been born first. She had started first for the world, and he had come on *bee*hind her, and so she was his eldest sister. Evidently the Debbil-debbils allow you to talk to your eldest sister.

When I asked what would happen if he turned a corner suddenly, and, without meaning to, saw his 'little-bit-somebody-he-shouldn't,' he answered wisely:

'Spose me shut him eye quickfellow, that all right.'

'Ebimel Wooloomool,' I said, giving him his full name, which always pleased him, 'you blackfellows plenty savey.'

He smiled a kingly smile at this, and when I asked him if he would like some flour to make a damper for his supper said, 'Dank you please, Missus,' and followed me to the store with a dirty old 'billy-can' in his hand. I gave him some flour and he carried it down to his camp-

-fire at the creek. In five minutes he was back with it. 'Missus,' he said, looking the very picture of misery, 'me bin spill him water longa flour; damper no good now,' and he held out his billy-can, and showed me a fearful sloppy-looking wet mess.

'Dear me!' I said, 'you've put too much water into it.'

'You eye,' he whined, 'me bin spilt him, Missus.'

'Never mind,' I said, 'I'll stiffen it up for you,' and he positively beamed, as I added some more flour. To my surprise, he was back again in a few minutes, saying:

'Missus! Me bin spill him nuzzer time.'

Then I saw what he was scheming for. He wanted a big damper.

'You old rogue,' I said, 'what do you mean, playing tricks on your Missus like this? You know you are doing it on purpose.'

He looked so astonished at being found out that I could not help laughing at him, and ended by stiffening his damper for him again.

He grinned into his tin with a very knowing air as he walked away, for he knew quite well that I was amused at his cuteness. When he reached the creek, he turned back to laugh at me, and I called:

'Good-bye, Goggle Eye; next time you spoil your damper, you can mend it by yourself.'

When Goggle-Eye reached the creek, he turned to laugh.

4

'Me King Alright'

How to punish Bett-Bett puzzled me more than anything. I often excused her naughty tricks because I thought she knew no better, but in certain things I was determined she should obey. The hardest work of all was to stop her from chewing tobacco. When I told her she must not, she smiled sweetly, and the very first chance she got begged pieces of 'chewbac' from the lubras.

Whipping her was no good, for I couldn't hurt her a little bit. I only seemed to tickle her.

'You too muchee little fellow, Missus!' she explained, cheerfully.

Any other punishment she got nothing but fun out of.

I gave her sewing to do, and she threaded ticks on to her needle and cotton.

I gave her bread and water for dinner, and she and Sue caught water-rats, and Bett-Bett made a fire and cooked them. In fact, they had a splendid picnic.

I took Sue away from her, and chained her up; but the little dog howled so dismally that I was more punished than Bett-Bett.

I shut her in the bath-room by herself. She always called it the 'bogey-house,' and she pretended that she was hiding from her enemies, and told Sue awful tales of Willeroo blacks, through the cracks under the door.

I could think of nothing else, and was at my wits' end; but the ever-cheerful Bett-Bett continued to chew tobacco.

Dilly bags used by Aboriginal women in the bush.

In despair, I had almost decided to send her back to the bush, when she suggested a fearful punishment herself, of course without meaning to do so.

I was busy painting some shelves one morning, and allowed Bett-Bett to help. She enjoyed it very much, and spattered herself and the ground for yards around with daubs of white. By and by the heat and the smell of the paint made us both sick. Bett-Bett was very bad, and thought she was going to die. 'Me close up dead-fellow, Missus,' she moaned. Poor little mite! she had never been sick before, and thought that her inside was coming right out. When she was well again, she asked me what had made her so ill, and I said it was the paint.

Next day she was singing like a young skylark, and chewing away at a piece of tobacco between times.

I was very angry indeed with her, and deciding to send her 'bush,' called sternly, 'Come here at once, Bett-Bett.'

To my surprise she screamed and cried out,

'No more, Missus. Me goodfellow; spose you no more make me whitefellow longa paint.'

I saw at once what she was afraid of. I had the paint-pot and brush in my hands, and she thought I was going to paint her, to make her sick for punishment. I put them down, and told her to come to me.

'Bett-Bett,' I said, 'will you be a good girl if I don't paint you this time?'

'You eye, Missus; straightfellow,' she sobbed.

'And you will not chew tobacco?' I added.

'No more, Missus; straightfellow,' she said, promising 'straightfellow,' or 'honour bright.'

'Very well,' I said, putting down the brush; 'I will not paint you today.' After that I had very little trouble with her, for the sight of the paint-pot made her as good as gold.

Bett-Bett loved polishing the silver, particularly the biscuit-barrel, which she called 'little-fellow billy-can belonga biscuit.' One morning we were busy with it on the verandah, when a shout from the lubras of 'Goggle Eye come on' made Bett-Bett scurry round the house like a young rabbit. It was always like this, and I began to wish the blacks would be less particular about falling in love with their relations.

As he came along, I saw he had a headache, for he had his wife's waist-belt round his head. It is wonderful how quickly a wife's belt or hair-ribbon will charm away a headache. It only fails when she has been up to mischief of any sort. Of course when a lubra's belt does not cure her husband, he knows she has been naughty, and punishes her as she deserves. The lubras say that the belts do not always speak the truth, but the men say they do. Whichever way it is, they are mean, horrid tell-tales.

I told Goggle Eye I was sorry for him, and as he really looked ill, I gave him a dose of Epsom salts to help the belt-cure, and to save Mrs. Goggle Eye, the Queen, from a beating. He took it, and then sitting down under the verandah, nursed his head in his hands—a poor forlorn old king! As he sat with his back to me, I saw a peculiar mark on his shoulder that I had not noticed before, and wondered what it meant.

All blackfellows have thick, ugly scars up and down and across their bodies and limbs, but Goggle Eye had more than most men.

He told me once that he had made a great many of them himself with a stone knife. After his first corrobboree he had cut himself a good deal to show the tribe that he was a man now, and not afraid of pain. Of course when any near relatives had died, he had cut himself all over his arms and thighs, to let the Spirit know that he was truly and properly sorry. Whenever a blackfellow dies, all his friends cut themselves a little, but his near relations gash themselves terribly, because if the Spirit thinks they are not sorry enough, he will very likely send Debbil-debbils along to punish them for their hardness of heart.

After a good long 'cry cry,' the wise men say that the Spirit is satisfied—I don't know how they tell—and then everybody rubs hot ashes into the wounds. This heals them very quickly, but it makes the scars into big ugly weals that will never fade away.

Goggle Eye would talk about this as often as I liked to listen, but whenever I asked him the meaning of the marks on his back or shoulders, he always answered, 'Nuzzing,' and either changed the subject or walked away.

Now when a blackfellow says 'Nuzzing' like that, it simply means that he is not going to tell, for when he really does not understand the meaning of a law or custom, he answers:

'All day likee that,' which means that his fathers did it, and so must he, even if he has forgotten why.

After a while, I saw Goggle Eye feeling among his thick curly hair for his pipe, and I guessed his headache was better. When he found it, he filled it ready for a smoke, and I remarked that Mrs. Goggle Eye must be a very good lubra. He smiled approval, and said, 'My Word!' and I thought that if Mrs. Goggle Eye had known everything, she would have given 'three cheers for good old Epsom!'

As he sat puffing at his pipe, I wondered if these extra marks had anything to do with his being King, but knew if I asked questions he would go away. Instead, I showed him a picture of King Edward VII, and told him that he wore a crown to show that he was King.

He liked this very much, and said so, and then smoked on in silence. At last, pointing to his right arm, he said:

'Me King alright,'

'My word!' I said, 'I think you big mob King.'

This pleased the vain old chap immensely.

'Me plenty savey corrobboree,' he chuckled, rubbing his hands up and down his back; 'me savey all about corrobboree.'

'My word!' I said, to show my great admiration. 'Tell me, Goggle Eye,' I added.

He hesitated for a while, and then told me that when a blackfellow has been through a corrobboree, his teachers put a mark on him, to show that he understands all about it—a certificate for the examination, I suppose! Of course a great number of marks mean a great deal of knowledge; so it was no wonder that Goggle Eye was proud of his. As he felt his certificates he chuckled, 'Big mob sit down longa me.'

Corrobborees are really the books of a tribe, for they have no

Aboriginals' spears and boomerangs.

others. They are not just dancing picnics, as some people think, but lessons, and very hard lessons too, sometimes.

The old men are the teachers, and the Head Man is the Head Master. They teach the young men all they should know—how to point 'death-bones,' the best way to 'sing' people dead, the way to scare Debbil-debbils away with bull roarers and sacred stones, all the laws about marriage, the proper things to eat, how to make rain, and I can't tell what else.

The man who proves in a great many ways that he understands all he should, will one day be King and Head Master. A black king is not king because his father was so.

As I listened to Goggle Eye's explanation of all this, I thought how necessary it was to have a wise king, since he has the care of the special 'death-bones,' and 'pointing-sticks,' and all the sacred charms. No one knows what terrible things might happen to the tribe if any one touched these magic charms who did not know how to use them. Why, he might set a death-bone working, and not be able to stop it till everybody was dead, or make a mistake and invite Debbil-debbils to come and chivvy everybody about, when he was meaning to tell them to stay away. It really is too fearful to think what might happen with a foolish king!

When Goggle Eye stopped talking, I asked him what the peculiar marks on his shoulder meant.

'What name this one talk, Goggle Eye?' I said, touching it with my finger.

He was just trying to decide whether it would be all right to tell a white woman what a black lubra must not hear, when a wretched little Willy-Waggletail flew into the verandah after spiders.

No blackfellow will talk secrets with one of these little birds about. They say they are the tell-tales of the bush, and are always spying about, listening for bits of gossip to make mischief. They call them 'Jenning-gherries,' or mischief-makers, and say that they love mischief of all kinds.

'Jenning-gherrie come on,' said Goggle Eye, pointing to the

little flitting, flirting bird, and I knew I should hear no more that day.

'Very well,' I said, and giving him a stick of 'chewbac,' sent him back to his camp, and called Bett-Bett.

She came, carrying old 'Solomon Isaacs,' our white cockatoo, on her wrist, and asked me why he had not got any legs.

'But he has,' I said. 'He has two,' and I touched them to show her.

'No, Missus,' she said, 'him hands,' and to prove that they were hands, she showed me that he was holding a biscuit in one of them as he nibbled at it.

'Perhaps he has one leg and one hand,' I suggested, saying that it was his leg he was standing on, and that his hand was the one with the biscuit in it.

That satisfied her, and she was just going off to play, when the miserable creature changed its biscuit into the other claw.

'Him twofellow hands, Missus,' she said, coming back to argue it all out again. Fortunately 'cocky' changed the subject, by passing a few remarks about himself and the weather. Bett-Bett listened for a while, and then informed me that a white man's spirit had jumped into 'Solomon Isaacs' when he was born, and that was why he could talk. Billy Muck knew, and had said so.

Before I could think of anything to say, the gramaphone in the men's quarters began to play, and she and Cocky went off to listen, and I had a little peace. When she came back she told me that a 'White Missus' and some whitefellow bosses were in the men's rooms. I wondered whoever they could be, for 'White Missuses' were rather scarce 'out bush,' and I hurried over to the quarters to make the lady welcome. I found no one there excepting the stockmen, and they said that no travellers at all had arrived, not even men.

I called Bett-Bett and asked where she had seen the 'White Missus' and the travellers. She said she hadn't seen them, she had only heard them singing.

'Him there, Missus,' she said, pointing to the gramaphone. 'I bin hear him sing-sing.' Then she wanted to know how they had got in, and what they had to eat, 'Which way whitefellow sit down, Missus?' she

Goggle Eye's belt and tassel.
Heads of Corroboree sticks, or Bull-roarers, presented to
"Missus" after the "Debbil-Debbil Dance."

asked, peering down the funnel of the gramaphone, and screwing up her comical little nose as she tried to shut one eye.

'I don't know, Bett-Bett,' I said, tired of answering questions. 'Come for a walkabout in the paddocks.'

Off she scampered to collect the lubras, and by the time I arrived at the gate, they were all waiting for me with their 'dilly bags.' I was the pupil, and they were the teachers, and my lessons were most interesting. They tried to teach me the tracks of animals, how to tell if they were new or old, where every bird built its nest, what it built it of, and how many eggs it laid, where to look for crocodiles' eggs, and where the Bower-bird danced. They knew the tracks of every horse on the run, and every blackfellow of the tribe, and if they came on a stranger's track, they knew the tribe he belonged to. They tried hard to teach me this, but try as I would, I could never see any difference, excepting in the size. They were very patient teachers, and I tried my very best; but I suppose I had not a blackfellow's sight for tiny differences, and I failed dismally, I couldn't even learn the tracks of my own lubras.

We all enjoyed the walkabout, and generally had a good time. This afternoon we found all sorts of queer prizes, and were coming home with them, when we came on Goggle Eye's tracks, going in our homeward direction.

Bett-Bett simply refused to go any further, and so we had to take a short cut through the scrub. By bad luck we came on his Majesty himself, just as we came up from the creek. He and Bett-Bett shut their eyes at once, and felt their way with outstretched hands. The path was very narrow, and as they groped about, I wondered what would happen if they bumped together, Perhaps Debbil-debbils would have come with a whizz, and would have left nothing but a little smoke!

5

'Goodfellow Missus'

It was washing-day, and we were all delighted. So would you have been if you had been there; for when washing is done by black lubras the fun is always fast and furious.

Directly after breakfast, which was usually at sunrise, there was a wild scramble among the bundles of soiled clothes, followed by a go-as-you-please race to the billabong or water-hole. Each lubra, as she ran, looked like a big snowball with twinkling black legs; while perched on top of two or three of the snowballs sat little shiny-black piccaninnies. Bett-Bett had not had many washing-days, and that accounts for her being last with the stocking-bag. As they reached the creek every one dropped her bundle, slipped off her clothes and began the day's work by taking a header into the water.

When I came along I threw big pieces of soap at them, and they all ducked and dived to dodge it, and when they came up they all ducked and dived again to find it.

'Now,' I said, sitting down in the shade of some pandanus palms, 'come and begin, and wash the clothes very clean to-day.'

'You eye, Missus,' they all answered, as they scrambled out up the banks.

'And don't play too much,' I added. At least, what I really did say was, 'No more all day play-about.'

'You eye, Missus,' they all said again, but grinned at each other. They knew as well as I did that as long as the work was well done, I would let them play over it as much as they liked. You see, I was what white people would call a 'bad mistress;' but the blacks called me a 'goodfellow

Missus,' and would do anything I wanted without a murmur.

They began to sort the clothes very seriously; but before half-a-minute had passed Bett-Bett and Judy were having a tug-of-war with a sheet, and everybody else was standing up to scream and shout. It was most exciting, particularly when Bett-Bett suddenly let go, and Judy and sheet took a double somersault into the water. As soon as her head came up every one pelted her with soap, which was the first thing that came handy. Then of course they all had to dive in to find it before they could go on with the washing. There is one thing a blackfellow can do perfectly, and that is to make hard work into play.

After all sorts of pranks, the clothes were sorted, and then every one climbed along an old tree trunk that had fallen into the water. There they sat, six naked lubras in a row, and rubbed and scrubbed and soaped, till the clothes looked like wet frothy balls, and the tree trunk was as slippery as an eel.

As they scrubbed, they kept up a perpetual sort of pillow fight with sloppy balls of clothes, knocking each other off the tree, till often there were more Lubras in the water than out of it. It certainly is a good plan to take your clothes off on washing-day in the tropics.

When everything was washed, the rinsing began; and if you like real fun, it's a pity you were not there.

The sheets and big things were done first. After they had been carefully spread out on top of the water, every one climbed up the banks and took flying leaps into them. Down they went to the bottom wrapped up in a sheet or tablecloth, there to kick and splash till they came to the top again. The first person out of the tangle ducked the others as they came up, or else swam off up the creek with a sheet, which still had one lubra half rolled up in it, and two or three others hanging on to it.

And the babies? The little shiny-black piccaninnies? They just played and rolled over each other on the banks. Every now and then one would roll into the water, only to swim out again, or to dogpaddle after its mother.

And what were Sue and I doing all this time? We were sitting in the warm, pleasant shade, enjoying the washing circus, and wondering why everybody wasn't drowned three or four times over. Blackfellows evidently can't drown.

When the rinsing was finished, and the clothes were 'cooking,' as we called boiling, the lubras put on their dresses and came and sat down near me. They knew well enough that I should have something good for them to eat. Canned fruit or sweet biscuit were always voted 'goodfellow,' but there was nothing so good as treacle—'blackfellow sugarbag,' you know.

It was treacle to-day, and as every one lay laughing, smoking and resting, the tin was passed round and round. Very thin, bony, black fingers went in, and very fat, juicy black fingers came out, and were put into grinning, happy mouths, Sue getting a lick from Bett-Bett's, every turn.

'Do you like washing-days, Bett-Bett?' I asked, as she sat waiting for another dig into the tucker.

'My word!' she grinned, dragging a crawling piccaninny from the treacle-tins by its legs.

Biddy interfered at once, by putting the baby's little fist into the sticky stuff. It was her piccaninny, you see, and engaged to be married to Goggle Eye!

'Biddy,' I said, as she bent forward to push the baby's treacly fingers into its open mouth, 'haven't you cut your hair rather short?' I had noticed the day before how pretty and curly it was, but now it was like a convict's.

'Goggle Eye bin talk,' she answered, meaning that he had told her to cut it. That was all she said, for she knew I would understand, you see; she was Goggle Eye's mother-in-law, and so all her hair or most of it belonged to him. Whenever it grew nice and long, he told her to cut it off and make him some string, and she had to obey. It was a bit of a nuisance being a mother-in-law.

I'm sure Billy Muck often wished that I was his mother-in-law, for he saw me drying my hair in the sun one day, and knew it was nice and long.

'My word, Missus!' he said, 'big mob hair sit down longa you cobra,' meaning, 'what a lot of hair you've got on your head.' Just think what lovely belts and things he would have ordered me to make, if only I had been his mother-in-law; but I wasn't, and I'm sure Billy Muck was the only person who was really sorry about it.

Bett-Bett was Jimmy's mother-in-law. Of course she wasn't married yet, only engaged to Billy Muck; but that did not matter. She was Jimmy's mother-in-law, and when she did grow up and have a piccaninny, it was to be his wife. In the meantime, nobody else could have her spare hair.

Common string is all right for common things, but charms and belts and special things must have hair-string, or they won't keep Debbil-debbils away properly. This way of having the mother-in-law's hair divides the hair of the tribe very evenly, as every man has two or three mothers-in-law.

When the treacle was finished, Sue began to dig a hole to lie down in. As she dug, she scratched up a little red and yellow worm. With a yell all the lubras grabbed hold of the poor little dog, and nearly pulled her in pieces in their hurry to get her away. Then they all shrieked and jabbered, and pointed at the scraggy wriggling thing, while Sue sat just where they had thrown her, too astonished to move.

'Well,' I said, 'that worm won't eat us, will it?'

'Him Rainbow Debbil-debbil,' they shrieked, shaking with fear at Sue's narrow escape.

'Nonsense,' I said; 'it's only a worm.'

But they insisted that it was a baby Rainbow.

'Him piccaninny Rainbow alright,' they cried.

'Don't be so silly,' I said, and bent forward to pick it up in my fingers; but they yelled their very best at this, and caught hold of my arms.

'Very well,' I said; 'come and tell me all about it, and what a baby Rainbow is doing down here.'

We all moved to a place of safety, and they explained that what we call hailstones are really Rainbow's eggs, and that they fall on the ground and hatch into worms— I mean baby Rainbows! The wise men of the tribe say it is so, and of course they know everything. This is how they found out: —many years ago a great number of hailstones fell, which is a very unusual thing on the Roper River; every one was afraid to touch them for they didn't know what they were; so they sat and looked at them in wonder until they had all burrowed into the ground—'melted,' the whites call it! Now this looked very strange, and after a great deal of talking, one very brave old blackfellow dug a hole to see what was happening underneath. Instead of hailstones, he found brightly-coloured little creatures—worms, of course—creeping about in the wet earth. Every one looked at them and said they were very like little Rainbows, and that they must have hatched out of the hailstones, which could be nothing else but Rainbow's eggs. Of course everybody knew, before, that the grown-up Rainbow is a Debbil-debbil snake who lives in the Roper River, and that he kindly takes care of the fish supply for the blackfellows. He is very good, and allows you to catch as many fish as you can eat, but he can't bear to see any wasted. He gets dreadfully angry if he knows that any one has been spearing fish for fun, and leaving them to rot on the banks. I don't wonder at his anger, for if everybody did that, soon there would be no fish left.

He and his wife often go for a stroll together in the sky. He is red and yellow in colour, and she is blue. It is while they are strolling about that they catch the guilty people. They pick them up before they can say 'Jack Robinson,' and carry them off to the Roper River—and feed the fish upon their bodies.

When I heard that the worm was really a baby Rainbow, I felt very thankful that I had not hurt it, for it would be awful to be chased by an angry Mother Debbil-debbil Rainbow!

After such a narrow escape we thought that under the palm trees was not a very safe place, so we went and finished the washing and spread everything out to dry, and then began the fun of chasing the grasshoppers, lest they should settle on the clothes and eat holes in them. As the lubras darted about, here and there, the scene looked more like a Sunday-school picnic than a washing-day. It certainly sounded like one.

Blacks are blacks, and whites are whites, and as I looked from the merry black faces to the clean white clothes, I knew their way of working was best—for them, at any rate, so I kept on being a 'bad mistress' and a 'goodfellow Missus,' and we all enjoyed washing day —all except Sue! The fun was too wet for her, and besides it always made her think of worms—Rainbows, I mean!

My friends used to wonder why I was not lonely, a hundred miles from any white neighbours, and I used to wonder if any one could be lonely with a perpetual circus and variety show on the premises.

Dressing for the Debbil-Debbil Dance.

6

The 'Debbil-Debbil' Dance

We were going to a Debbil-debbil dance. The King himself had brought the invitation to me in the garden.

'Missus,' he said, 'spose you come longa Debbil-debbil dance, eh?'

'No, thank you, Goggle Eye,' I answered. 'Might it the Debbil-debbils carry me off?'

He roared with delight at my joke and explained, 'this one gammon Debbil-debbil.'

'Oh well,' I said, 'if you are only going to have gammon Debbil-debbils at your party, I come.'

'Dank you please, Missus,' he said, guessing at my meaning.

Then he asked if I would go and see the dancers being dressed for the performance, and I said I would, for I always like to see a blackfellow getting into clothes of any sort. I went in the afternoon and watched, noticing directly I arrived that two of the gentlemen had headaches. Poor Bett-Bett had to stay at home because of Goggle Eye. It took two or three men to dress one dancer properly. They laid him flat on his back to begin with, and pricked him all over with sharp stones and pieces of glass. As they sat pricking Billy Muck, they reminded me of cooks pricking sausages for frying.

When little beads of blood oozed out, they were smeared all over the man, face and all. Then tiny white cockatoo's feathers were stuck up and down and round and round him, and the blood was used as gum. They made wonderful patterns all over his body, back and front, ending up with twirligigs down both arms and legs. The gum stuck splendidly;

Making his legs look exactly like the figure "4".

if you want to find out how well blood sticks, cut your finger and tie it up with cotton wool.

The face also was covered with down, and a huge helmet, with a long horn of emu's quills, was fixed firmly on the head.

The finishing touch was a wreath of leaves at each ankle. Ordinary leaves were not nearly good enough for a Debbil-debbil dance. So special magic men, and some extra special lubras, went 'out bush,' and bewitched a tree with all sorts of capers, and prancings, and pointings and magic. Then they gathered some leaves and carried them in for the dancers to wear. It was wise to do this, for then nothing could possibly go wrong with the corroboree.

By the time everybody was dressed, they looked truly awful; and I pleased them immensely by pretending to be frightened of these 'gammon Debbil-debbils.'

I begged them not to carry me off, and they shouted with delight, and waved sticks at me, and danced about and said, 'Me Debbil-debbil alright, me real fellow,' and tried hard to look fierce in spite of their grins. Poor old Goggle Eye was nearly bent double with laughing; for if there is one thing a blackfellow likes better than anything else it is a 'play-about,' as they call fun and nonsense.

After supper we arrived at the party—four white men and a woman! The moon had risen, and innumerable fires were flickering among the trees; and everything was ready to begin.

His Majesty the King, and the Lords in Waiting, received us with a broad grin. Then they each stood on one leg and chuckled. Whenever a blackfellow has nothing better to do with his legs, he always stands on one, and lays the sole of the other foot against his knee, making his legs look exactly like the figure 4, with an extra long stem. I think our hosts chuckled because they did not know what else to do.

I thought, perhaps, that some of the old men might not be too pleased to have me at the party, and I said so to Goggle Eye. 'Me bin talk,' he answered, with a wave of his hand, that showed he was in every way King.

The lubras were sitting near, ready to sing and beat time for the dancers. I think in the excitement of getting ready for the party, they must have forgotten to dress themselves, for they had nothing on, excepting a few feathers and things that had been left over from the men's costumes. As nobody seemed to notice this, I suppose it did not matter.

A great big place had been cleared of all sticks and stones, and the whole tribe and their visitors stood round it, armed with spears. This particular patch of ground was near to a very sacred stone, and unless this corroboree was danced there it would not be of much good. That was why it was so near the homestead.

The lubras began to sing a strange weird song, and a few blackfellows sounded the bamboo trumpets, and then the dancing commenced. It was very tiring both to dancers and onlookers. Up every one lifted a leg, and down every one stamped a leg and gave a fearful yell; then Billy Muck, who was a little way off from the dancers, gave a jump and a little run—and that was the First Figure!

Up went the legs again, and down went the legs again; we heard another yell, and Billy Muck gave another jump and run—and that was the Second Figure.

The Third Figure was just the same, and so were the Fourth, Fifth, Sixth, and as many more as you liked to count.

'What name, Goggle Eye?' I asked, meaning that I wished him to explain it to me.

He said this was to teach the young men of the tribe that Debbil-debbils would chase them if they did wrong. You see the dancers were supposed to be fearful Debbil-debbils and were pretending to catch Billy Muck. They kept acting this object lesson for nearly two hours, and the old men explained what it meant to the pupils, but I got very tired of it.

I amused myself with watching the lubras as they sang and swayed about, noticing after a while that Bett-Bett was among them, singing and swaying and having a real good all-round time. She must have crept along after us, but as she was sitting with her back to Goggle Eye and his eyes were fixed on the dancers, I suppose it was all right. Anyway no Debbil-debbils came along.

Suddenly there was a wild weird shriek, quite near us. It came so unexpectedly, and was so unearthly, that I jumped and thought of Bett-Bett and Goggle Eye and Debbil-debbils. Everything was so strange around us, that I believe if they had been carried off I should have looked on without any surprise.

Every one stopped singing and dancing, and Goggle Eye whispered that it was the voice of the great sacred Bullroarer, calling to say that it was time to take the young boys away into the bush. There were four or five of them at this corroboree, and they were to be taught their first real lesson to-night. After it they would be kept away by themselves, in a special camp 'out bush,' and when they came back they would be treated as men.

The Bullroarer is a spindle-shaped piece of sacred stone, and when swung round and round above the head with a string, it shrieks and screams and groans. Only the wise men may touch it, and of course they are the only people who really understand all it says. Every man has an imitation bullroarer, which he often swings to make it speak, for this pleases the Debbil-debbil spirit of the sacred Bullroarer. After the voice of the Debbil-debbil had spoken, a few of the very important people began to slip away, to prepare for the real corroboree; for the dance was only a sort of introduction.

Goggle Eye gave us a hint to go home, and we took it; we had our revolvers with us, but it is always wise to take a blackfellow's hint, particularly when he says that a very secret, sacred corroboree is about to begin.

As we said good-night, Goggle Eye and old Jimmy presented me with two extraordinary-looking broad flat sticks, with black streaks and white dots on them.

'Him goodfellow-stick, that one,' they explained, and it was not till some time after that I found out they had paid me the very highest compliment a blackfellow can pay a 'white missus,' for no ordinary woman is allowed even to look at these sticks.

I often wish I had said 'Dank you, please,' a little more politely and gratefully for them. A few mornings after the Debbil-debbil Dance, I saw Goggle Eye hide something behind an ant-bed, and then walk up to the house. When he saw me he asked if he might 'go bush' for a walk about, as he was needed at a corrobboree at Duck Creek. I asked him how long he would be away and he said, 'One fellow, two fellow, big mob sleep,' meaning that he would be away for a great number of nights or sleeps before he had finished his business.

Then he showed me a little bit of stick with notches on it, and said it was a blackfellow's letter-stick, or as he called it, a 'yabber-stick.' It was round, not flat like most other letters, and was an invitation to a corroboree, and there were notches on it explaining what sort of corroboree it was, and saying that it was to be held at Duck Creek. There was some other news marked on it which Goggle Eye told me, and then he sold it to me for some 'chewbac,' and I have it to-day, and anyone may see it who wishes. Then he sat down for a yarn, and I asked him why Jackeroo would never eat turkey, and why he always said he mustn't eat it, because it was his brother.

Goggle Eye said, that was quite right, and that turkeys *were* Jackeroo's brothers, for he and turkeys both had turkey spirits inside them, and of course no one could eat his brother. Everybody has the spirit of some animal inside him, he said. If you have a kangaroo spirit, you belong to the kangaroo family or totem; and you must not eat your brothers the kangaroos. If you have a snake's or an eagle's spirit you belong to the snake's or eagle's family, and do not eat your brothers the snakes or the eagles. Whatever spirit you may have, you belong to its family or totem, and they are your brothers, and you do not eat them. 'All day likee that,' said old Goggle Eye.

I asked him how each person knew which spirit was inside him, and he said that their mothers told them. You see, she knew where she had 'caught' her piccaninny. If a piccaninny came to her in a snake's-spirit country, it had a snake spirit, and if it came to her in a kangaroo's-spirit country, it had a kangaroo's spirit, and so on. It all depended on where you came from. It didn't matter what your mother and father were; your mother might have a snake's spirit, and your father might have a wallaby's spirit; but if you came from a cockatoo's-spirit country, you had to have a cockatoo's spirit; just as peaches come from peach trees, and plums from plum trees.

Near the homestead was the kangaroo's-spirit country, and of course all the children who came from there had kangaroos' spirits, but those who came from the Long Reach, not a mile away, had honey-bees' spirits.

Goggle Eye said you learnt all this at corroborees. At the kangaroo-corroboree the head man of the kangaroo men dressed up, and pretended to be a kangaroo. After a little while he suddenly changed into a man, and stood up, and looked like one, and said he really was a man now. Then he dug a little hole and poured water into it. After this he called a number of kangaroo-spirit men to him and offered them the flesh of a kangaroo, but they said it was the flesh of their brother, and that they must not eat it.

The wise men then explained that this was to teach them that once, long long ago, a big giant kangaroo had come to the Roper River country, and changed himself into a man. When he got thirsty he dug a hole, and water flowed up into it for him to drink, and that was really how the homestead 'billabong' came.

After a while this kangaroo man amused himself with making spirits, but as he was really a kangaroo spirit himself, he could only make kangaroo spirits. By and by he noticed that some of them had got into kangaroos and some into little black children, so he called them all together and told them that they all had kangaroo spirits and were really brothers and must never eat each other.

After this explanation all the young men of the tribe understood of course that they must not eat their animal brothers. At honey-bee-corroborees, the history of the honey-bees was taught, and at each animal corroboree, the history of each totem, for corroborees, as I said before, were the schools of the blackfellows.

Goggle Eye, you see, was one of the wisest of the blackfellows, and as he said this was true, perhaps it was. I know that 'out-bush' we had seen portraits of the great-great-greatest grandfather of the Kangaroo men, and of the Fish and of the Iguana people, drawn on rocks and trees by the artists of the tribe.

When Goggle Eye had finished his history lesson, I gave him some sugar in a calico bag, and he tied it carefully round his neck. He said the ants couldn't get at it there. Then I gave him a red handkerchief and some tobacco and hairpins. The blacks love hairpins, they find them so useful to dig up grubs with.

As Goggle Eye still stayed about, I said good-bye, and turned to leave him.

'Missus,' he called after me, 'me bin lose 'em pipe.' Something in his face made me suspicious. I went and looked behind the antbed to see what he had hidden, and found his pipe.

'Here you are, Goggle Eye,' I said; 'me bin good fellow, me bin find him.'

I expected him to look ashamed of himself, but he didn't—not a little bit! He sat down and laughed till the tears rolled down his cheeks at the joke of it all, and that made me laugh too. Of course in the end Goggle Eye got a new pipe, and went off 'bush' with it in his mouth. As he went through the gate he turned and waved it at me, and that was the last time I saw him looking merry-hearted and happy.

The 'great-great -greatest grandfather of the Kangaroo Men, and the Iguana Men', as drawn by Aboriginal artists on rocks.

7

'Mumma A' and 'Mumma B'

I had taught Sue some tricks—to beg, shake hands, and pretend to be 'deadfellow'—and Bett-Bett was wild with delight.

'My word, Missus!' she cried excitedly, 'Sue plenty savey, him close up whitefellow.' Then seizing her darling in her arms, she darted off to the humpy to show her to the lubras, singing as she ran, 'Sue plenty savey; him savey, him savey!'

When they came back I was reading, and paid no attention to them.

After a while Bett-Bett said—

'What name, Missus?'

I looked up to see her staring very hard at me, with a puzzled look on her face.

'What name, what?' I said, wondering what she meant.

She did not answer at once, but picked up a book, and held it so close to her face that it almost touched her nose; then staring at it till her eyes nearly jumped out of her head, she said—

'What name, likee this? likee this? likee this?'

I laughed at her and said—

'Bett-Bett, I hope I don't look like that when I read,' for she looked a fearful little object. But I saw what was puzzling her; she could not understand why I sat looking so earnestly at little black marks on paper.

I explained that books could talk like 'paper yabbers,' as she called letters—papers that 'yabber,' or talk, you know.

Then I got a little ABC book, and some paper and pencils, and told her I would teach her to read; but it was easier said than done.

We began with the capital letters. Bett-Bett repeated 'A' after me, and made it on paper, and then wanted to know what it was. Was it tucker, or an animal, or somebody's name?

I sat looking so earnestly at little black marks on paper. 'What did the mark say?' she asked. 'What name him yabber, Missus, this one A?' were the exact words she used.

You remember that on Goggle Eye's letter-stick marks were cut, and that every mark had a special meaning; so Bett-Bett was sure that 'A' must be the name of something.

I couldn't explain it, so told her that when she knew all the names of the letters, I would tell her what they meant, and we went on to B.

The sound reminded Bett-Bett of bees and honey. 'Him sugar-bag,' she said, grinning at her cleverness. Then she made it in the dust with her toe, and told Sue— 'Him talk sugar-bag, this one B.' Sue looked wise and smelt it, and then offered to shake hands all round. And that was our first day's lesson.

Next day we learnt a few more letters, and capital 'I' was christened 'This one eye,' as a smutty little finger tapped Bett-Bett's eye.

A day or two afterwards 'W' was noticed on ahead.

'Missus,' she cried, pointing to it, 'I bin find bullocky.'

'What name?' I said, wondering what was coming now.

'Bullocky,' she repeated, nodding her head wisely at 'W' and then 'him all day sitdown longa bullocky.'

Then I understood her. 'W' was the letter of the station brand, and she had seen it on the cattle and remembered it.

We plodded on day after day, and every day Bett-Bett gave me a hint that she did not think much of lessons.

'Me knock up longa paper yabber, Missus; him silly fellow,' she kept saying.

I took no notice of her remarks, but I think the only thing either of us learnt was patience.

The capitals were bad enough, but when we began the little letters, things got dreadfully mixed.

'Me savey,' she said, pointing from one to the other.

'This one mumma; this one piccaninny.' Then she wanted to know the baby's name; what its mother called it. She said that piccaninnies always had different names to their mummas.

Of course I didn't know the baby's name, and told her so. Very often there was no answer to Bett-Bett's questions; but somehow she always made me feel that it was my fault, or my ignorance, that there wasn't. After this we said: 'Mumma A and piccaninny belonga mumma A; mumma B and piccaninny belonga mumma B, and so on to the very end of the alphabet, till our tongues ached.

On the page Bett-Bett was learning from, every little letter was next to its mother. Little 'a' next mumma 'A,' and little 'b' next mumma 'B'; but in the reading lessons little letters were walking about by themselves. One day she noticed this when she was looking through the book.

'Look, Missus!' she cried, excitedly. 'Piccaninny belonga mumma 'A' sit down by meself.' Then she scolded the little letter dreadfully, 'You go home longa you mumma,' she said, in a loud, angry voice, shaking her finger at it. But small 'a' never moved; it just sat and looked at her, and Bett-Bett told me it was 'cheeky fellow longa me,' meaning it was not at all afraid of her. 'My word! you badfellow alright,' she went on, scolding hard; 'Debbil-debbil catch you dreckly.' As little 'a' took no notice of this awful threat, she turned back to tell 'mumma A' about its naughty piccaninny. There she found that the little letter had slipped home, and was sitting quietly at its mother's knee. She was so pleased about it, 'Look, Missus,' she said, coming to show me; 'him goodfellow now.'

'It's a very good little letter,' I said, 'and you're a good little lubra, and may go and help to water the garden.'

She gave a piercing, ear-splitting yell of delight, and called Sue; but before she went asked me if the little 'a' in my book was good.

I said 'Yes,' and hoped I was telling the truth; as far as I knew, they were good. I suppose Bett-Bett thought I spent hours sending naughty piccaninnies home to their mummas. Almost before I knew that she and Sue had gone, I heard shrieks from the vegetable garden, and yells of 'Missus! Missus!' and Biddy and Rosey came running through the open gate. 'What's the matter now?' I said, as I went to meet them, for there was always something fresh happening.

'Missus!' they panted, 'Bett-Bett bin kill Rolly; him bin kill him longa quart pot.'

I waited to hear no more, but ran as fast as I could to the garden, with the lubras at my heels; hoping that Rolly was not really dead, but perhaps only stunned.

The first thing I saw was Bett-Bett and Rolly quietly watering the garden.

'You naughty lubras,' I said, turning sharply to Biddy and Rosey; 'what do you mean, telling such wicked stories? What name you all day gammon, eh?' for I was very angry indeed with them; they had given me a terrible fright.

To my surprise, they insisted that Bett-Bett had killed Rolly.

'Straightfellow, Missus,' they said earnestly; 'Bett-Bett bin kill Rolly alright.' Even Rolly herself said: 'Bett-Bett bin kill me, Missus! Straightfellow! Me no more talk gammon.'

But Bett-Bett herself said nothing; she kept on watering the garden, with one eye on the Missus. I suppose she was thinking of the paint-pot.

'You silly things,' I said, feeling very puzzled, for they were in deadly earnest. 'Can't you see that Rolly is not deadfellow?'

At this everybody shouted with laughter. At last they understood the Missus and her anger.

'Me no more bin talk kill him deadfellow,' they screamed. 'Me bin talk kill him longa quart pot.'

So they had. I remembered now, and as usual it was my fault. Nobody but the Missus ever seemed to do anything wrong. I should have understood their funny 'pidgin English' better. To 'kill' only means to hit, or prick, or thump; but to put some one actually to death is to 'kill deadfellow.' Only that morning Bett-Bett had said, when her needle pricked her finger, 'My word, Missus! neenel bin kill finger belonga me.'

I called Bett-Bett, and asked her what she had been doing.

She said that when she got to the garden, she had found Rolly using her favourite quart pot to sprinkle water with. She had asked for it, but Rolly would not give it up, so she had hammered her with another to make her. 'Me bin long time kill him,' she said, but as Rolly wouldn't give in, Biddy and Rosey had run for me to stop the quarrel. Of course, when they saw me coming Rolly had dropped the quart pot and Bett-Bett had stopped 'killing' her, and they had both gone on with the watering.

That was all. Such a fuss about nothing! I took the leaky old quart pot from them, and sending them all back to their work, sat down under the banana clump.

In five minutes they were shouting merrily and playing practical jokes on one another; for with a blackfellow, as soon as a quarrel is over, it is forgotten.

Watering the garden is something like washing-day —plenty of fun and water, and very few clothes.

The fun began when Rosey went to fill her bucket. Judy and Biddy caught her by the heels and sent her flying into the billabong. As she scrambled out they 'showered' her from full buckets and quart pots, and then ran screaming and spluttering up the banks. Rosey waited her chance, and soon sent Biddy headlong into the pumpkin bed, with a bucket of water after her. Judy screamed with delight at this, only to get a full quart of water into her gaping, shouting mouth. Bett-Bett had thrown it, but in her hurry to dodge the watermelon that Judy flung back at her, tripped and sat down in her own bucket of water, and Rolly got the watermelon in the middle of her back. It broke into a dozen pieces, and of course that meant a wild scramble for the red, juicy fruit, and then everybody sat down to enjoy it properly, and flipped the pips into each other's faces.

They played these pranks every night, and kept the water flying in all directions; but as it always ended by falling somewhere among the vegetables, the garden was a great success, for it was always well watered. As I said before, a blackfellow sees no sense in working when play will do as well. As I sat watching them, and expecting a shower-bath every minute or two, Jimmy came along, whittling a bit of stick.

'What name, Jimmy?' I asked.

'Yabber stick,' he answered shortly, and squatting down near me, cut busily on.

'What name him talk?' I said, for that was the way to ask him what message he was cutting.

Jimmy spat thoughtfully on the ground and looked wise, but said nothing; and I saw I would have to flatter him a little before he would tell me much. He dearly loved to be important, and generally had to be coaxed and flattered a good deal.

'My word, Jimmy!' I said; 'you plenty savey. Me no more savey yabber stick.' This pleased him immensely, so I added, 'I think you close up savey white-fellow paper-yabber, Jimmy.'

He grinned from ear to ear with delight, and then taking the letter stick in one hand, and pointing at it with his pipe, began to instruct the poor ignorant Missus.

Jimmy looked very gay to-day. He had a small Union Jack flag hanging from his belt like a little apron. His dilly-bag was decorated with strips of red turkey twill and bunches of white feathers, and he had tied a little mussel shell on to the end of every bobbing curl of his head, and they danced and jingled as he talked.

'This one stick him yabber boomerang,' he began, pointing to a little mark like a V drawn sideways— so <.

I looked carefully at it, and then Jimmy spat once or twice before he explained that when that mark 'sat down' on a 'yabber stick,' it meant you were being asked for the loan of a boomerang. Then he spat again, and took a few pulls at his pipe, and looked very wise indeed.

'My word, Jimmy!' I murmured.

Jimmy grinned, and then showed me all sorts of marks which he drew in the dirt with his finger. Signs for spears, food, wet season, people's names, white men, names of places, and many other things. He ended up with 'chewbac' and his own name. He was very particular that I should remember 'chewbac.' Then he showed me a letter he had just received from Terrible Billy at Daly Waters. Jimmy's lubra Nellie was his mother-in-law, and this letter was to say that he was quite out of hair-string, and would Nellie kindly cut her hair and send some. All

Jimmy grinned, and then showed me all sorts of marks which he drew this was told in a winding line, twisting round and round the stick, and a short stroke to end with, and then Nellie's name, which read, 'String—long—hair—Nellie.' Then came some gossip—one thick ring which said 'walk-about,' and a mark which was Monkey's name. Now 'Monkey' was a Willeroo, and always up to mischief; so it was very kind of Billy to warn Jimmy that he was having a walk-about. Perhaps he was afraid that Monkey might run off with his mother-in-law, hair and all.

Jimmy's lecture was suddenly cut short by shrieks from the lubras of—

'Cheeky fellow snake sit down. Cheeky fellow snake, Missus.'

Jimmy ran to the cucumber bed, all his little shells bobbing and jingling as he went, and quick as a flash caught the snake by the tail, and broke its back by cracking it like a stock-whip, and then flinging it from him. In case of accidents, the lubras and I had all scurried in behind the bananas. It is just as wise to be out of the way when poisonous snakes are flying through the air; for of course a 'cheeky fellow snake' means a poisonous one.

After a good look at the horrid creature, we all went back to the house, leaving Jimmy to finish his letter. As we went, I saw that Bett-Bett was carrying the snake on the end of a long stick.

'What name, Bett-Bett?' I asked.

'Me put him longa Nellie bed,' she answered, grinning and going down to the humpy. Nellie was out, and Bett-Bett arranged the snake in a very life-like position on her bluey. Of course in about an hour we heard shrieks of 'Cheeky fellow snake sit down longa Nellie bed.' The Aboriginal world flew to the rescue, and Nellie got unmercifully teased for being frightened of a 'deadfellow snake'; while Bett-Bett grinned secretly and impishly.

Next morning Nellie brought me a 'yabber stick' cut all over with 'chewbac' signs, and with Jimmy's name at the bottom. I now understood why he wanted me to remember this sign, for the letter read— 'Jimmy wants a big mob of tobacco.' I saw the old rascal grinning through the trees, to see if I was understanding his joke. 'Jimmy,' I said, calling him up, 'you're the cutest, cleverest old black that ever was born, and you ought to be King. You know exactly how to manage your Missus.'

Jimmy seemed to think this was a compliment, and chuckled as I threw him a couple of sticks of 'chew-bac.' He picked them up with his toes, and passed them into his hands without bending his back. As he and Nellie walked away, I saw that she had obeyed her son-in-law, and had cut her hair.

There were a few old men at home...

8

A 'Walkabout'

'Go and lay 'em egg, silly fellow you. Go and lay 'em egg, silly fellow you,' shouted Bett-Bett in a singsong voice, as she and Sue dodged between an old broody hen and the tool-house.

Bett-Bett had no patience with broody hens; she seemed to think they were wasting their time; particularly when, like this one, they would try to hatch chickens out of nails. 'Come for a walk-about, Bett-Bett,' I called; 'I am going to the Long Reach for some water-lilies.'

'You eye, Missus,' she shrieked in answer, still dodging and dancing after old broody.

As I went for my hat and revolver, I heard her shrill little voice up at its highest pitch inviting every one within hearing to come with us. By the time I reached the slip-rails, there were six or eight lubras, a few piccaninnies, and about twenty dogs at my heels, and I felt like a Pied Piper of Hamelin.

We had a very merry walk-about that afternoon. Everything that could, seemed to happen. Just as we crossed the creek outside the slip-rails the fun began, and Sue got into trouble. She picked up the scent of a bandicoot, and was darting off to run its tracks, when her black legs were seized by Bett-Bett, and she got a ringing box on the ears.

She deserved it, for she was actually going to run tracks away from the direction in which the animal's toes were pointing. She should have noticed at once that the scent grew stronger the other way. Good little black dogs always do. Bett-Bett quickly put her right, and off everyone scampered after her, till she stopped at a hollow log. Bett-Bett and Sue arrived first, and everybody else immediately after, only to find that the bandicoot was not at home, for there were newer tracks leading out again. Sue simply couldn't believe it, and scratched wildly till stopped by another box on the ears. I was last to arrive, but came up just as the dogs scented the new tracks, and very soon afterwards the unfortunate bandicoot was hanging from one of the lubras' belts.

The Long Reach is a beautiful twelve-mile-long waterhole, full of crocodiles and water-lilies. It begins about three-quarters of a mile from the homestead, but we took nearly two hours to get there, for we zigzagged through the scrub, and had ever so many exciting hunts, several natural history lessons, and a peep into every nook and cranny we passed, to see how birds, beasts and insects made their nests.

Do you think if any one had seen me—a white woman with a revolver and cartridges at her belt, hunting with a mob of lubras—that they would have imagined that I was at school?

We had a strange lubra with us—one I had not seen before. I noticed that she dragged a leafy branch after her wherever she went. I asked her why she did this, and she told me that she had run away from her husband, and didn't want him to find her.

'Me knock up longa me boy,' she said, 'him all day krowl-krowl,'—she meant growl.

You see, he would of course travel about, looking at any tracks he came on, trying to find her, and so Murraweedbee—for that was her name—dragged this branch along after her like a rake, to scratch and mix up her tracks, so that nobody could possibly recognize them. Instead of disguising herself, she disguised her footprints.

When at last we arrived at the Reach, the lubras went into the water to gather lilies, and Bett-Bett and I poked about in the sand after crocodiles' eggs.

She would never hunt for these eggs on the Roper River. She said the sea-going crocodiles were 'cheeky fellow,' and would 'round you up' if you did.

Then she told me a thrilling experience she had had once. She had had once. She was scratching about on the banks of the Roper River and found a nest of eggs. She was just gathering them up, when she heard a splash, and saw the mother crocodile swimming across the river. 'My word! me race quickfellow,' she said, and she looked terribly frightened as she remembered how nearly she had been caught. She had evidently just seen the mother in time. Crocodiles in the land-locked pools were 'frightened fellow,' she said, so it was always safe to take their eggs. They were too timid to round you up.'

She scratched around for a while and then told me that 'crocodiles all day knock up longa egg,' meaning they could not be bothered with looking after them, but just left them to hatch in the sand, keeping one eye on them in case of accidents.

Bett-Bett was only eight years old, but what she didn't know about natural history was hardly worth knowing; but then she had the best teacher in all the world—Mother Nature. She never wearies her pupils, but punishes them pretty severely when they make mistakes. The most certain way of learning that crocodiles watch their eggs, and that sea-going crocodiles are fiercest, is to be chased by the mother. Bett-Bett certainly knew her lessons, which is more than can be said of many white children. They were only timid crocodiles in the Long Reach, and after a long hunt in the sand, we came on a nest of eggs, and Bett-Bett broke one, and, there all ready to hatch, we saw a tiny crocodile, curled up like a clock spring. These eggs are very curious; they seem to have two distinct shells and look exactly like a hen's egg inside a duck's egg.

The eggs we found were of no use for eating, so Bett-Bett covered them up again, keeping only one out, which she said would hatch next day. I asked her what she was going to do with it, but she only grinned impishly, and I knew she was up to some of her pranks.

As we went back to the lubras, we came on an old blackfellow, fishing in the water hole. He was standing on a tree trunk holding a spear, poised ready to dart at the first fish that came up to breathe. I called to him but he took no notice, and the lubras laughed and said he was 'Old No-More-Hearem,' and threw stones at him.

I called to them to stop, for I was afraid he would be angry with us, but they said he was deaf and dumb, and that every one threw stones

Old No-More-Hearum, fishing.

'Sea-going crocodiles were cheeky fellows'

at him when they wanted him to look round. I said this was rather painful for 'No-More-Hearem,' but they seemed to think it was his own fault for being deaf and dumb. Two or three of the stones hit him and he turned round. Then they all began talking in the sign language, asking the news and answering questions. The blacks' sign language is very perfect. They have a sign for every bird, beast, fish, person, place and action. They have long talks without uttering a word. There are many times when a blackfellow must not speak, unless by signs. For instance, if he is mourning for a near relative, or has just come from a very special corroboree. Often he must keep silent for weeks, and occasionally for months, and it is because of this and many other reasons that the sign language is so perfect. Every one can speak it, and every one does so when hiding in the bush from enemies, and then there is no fear of voices being heard.

It is very wonderful, but then the blacks are wonderful. To have any idea of how wonderful they are, you must live among them, going in and out of their camps, and having every one of them for a friend. Just living in a house that happens to be in a blackfellow's country is not living among blacks, although some people think it is.

We told old 'No-More-Hearem' to come for tobacco, and then we all started for home. Before very long Bett-Bett saw a bee's nest, and shouting out, 'sugar-bag,' as she thrust her crocodile's egg into my hand, began climbing a tree. Everybody climbed up after her to have a look, and then down again for sticks, and up again for the honey; poking at it with the long sticks and hanging on anywhere and everywhere like a troop of black monkeys. I waited below, and the dogs thinking it might perhaps be a 'possum hunt, danced about and barked ready to catch anything that came down. When all the honey was gathered into broad leaves, we went on home, calling in at the blacks' camp when we got there. There were a few old men at home, among them Billy Muck and an old bush black or 'myall.' Billy noticed at once that I had some tobacco and matches, and began puzzling his brains to think of some way of getting a piece without asking for it. To tease him I gave all the others a bit and pretended to start for home, as though I had forgotten him. Suddenly a bright idea struck him.

'Missus,' he called after me, 'spose me make you blackfellow fire, eh?'

I said I would very much like to see him make a blackfellow's fire, andnasked him where his matches were.

He grinned broadly at this and showed me two pieces of stick, with a little notch cut in one. I pretended to be very ignorant and asked what they were for.

Instead of answering he squatted down on the ground, and picking a few tiny pieces of dry grass, laid them in a little heap beside him; then laying one of his sticks on the ground near the grass, he held it firmly in place with his foot, and fixing one end of the other stick in the little notch or groove, twirled it quickly between the palms of his hands. In a few seconds some tiny tiny red-hot ashes, no bigger than grains of sand, were rubbed out. Billy bent over them, and blew softly till the grass took fire; then he stood on one leg and chuckled, and stuck his fire-sticks behind his ears.

It was all so quickly and cleverly done that I gave him two sticks of tobacco for payment, which pleased him immensely; but the old myall looked as though he were wondering what Billy had done to deserve so much 'chewbac.' Making a fire was nothing.

To see what he would do, I said—

'Billy Muck, I can make a fire quicker than you,' and striking a match on my shoe, I set fire to some grass. The myall ran forward eagerly to see how it was done, so I struck another and gave him a box for himself.

He sat down at once and was so fascinated with his new toy that he struck off all his matches one after the other, making little grass fires all around him, till he looked like a black Joan of Arc at the stake. When they were all gone he came and showed me the empty box, saying—

'Me bin finissem, Missus.'

I gave him some more and a stick of tobacco, and then followed Bett-Bett up to the house. I found her crocodile's egg lying on the garden path, and picking it up, hid it in the office. When she came back and found it gone, she gave one quick glance at the ground, and then walked to the office door and stopped. She was not allowed in there.

'Missus,' she said, 'which way you bin put him egg belonga crocodile?'

I said, 'You left it in the garden, Bett-Bett,' and suggested that perhaps Sue had carried it off. 'Might it Sue bin catch him, eh?'

'No more, Missus!' she said, grinning knowingly. 'You bin put him longa office. Track belonga you sit down,' she added, pointing at my footprints, leading from the garden to the office. I saw it was no use playing 'hide the thimble' with a little black girl who followed up my tracks, and I gave her back her precious egg. Once I had tried playing 'hide and seek' with the lubras; but I could never by any chance find them, and they always tracked me up, so it was not much fun. Their favourite way of hiding was to lie flat down in the grass, with their limbs spread out till they looked like open pairs of scissors, with grass growing between the handle and the blades. If you have ever looked for a hoop that has fallen in the grass, you will know how hard it was to find these lubras— how hard and how interesting.

When I gave Bett-Bett her egg, she took it to the broody hen, and filled her cup of happiness to the brim by letting her sit on it.

After supper, Bett-Bett threw herself down on the grass and said —'Me tired fellow alright, Missus,' and then she wanted to know why white people live in houses. I could not see any connection between these two ideas till she said, 'Him silly fellow likee that. Spose you tired fellow, what's the matter all day come home?' Then I understood what was the grievance. When a blackfellow is tired, and has plenty of tucker for supper, he sees no sense in walking a long way, just to sit on one particular patch of ground and call it home. When you have miles of beautiful country all your own, it is a much better plan to have your home just where you happen to be at the moment; and this can be arranged very easily, if you have nothing to carry about the world but a naked black body. When Bett-Bett lived 'out bush,' she told me that she and her friends would just wander about wherever they liked. If they grew tired, or the sun got too hot, they would lie down and go to sleep in the beautiful warm shade. When they woke up, very likely they would go down to the nearest water-hole and have a bogey. If it was a pleasant water-hole, and some other blacks happened to be there, they would stay a few days until the tucker

A Poolooloomee ready for the fire *(top left)*; Jimmy's Union Jack apron
(top right); Jimmy's 'gammon-stick, asking for tobacco.
'Tiny little wooden canoes, about two feet long, called Coolamuns'

began to get scarce, and then all start off together, to pay some friends a visit at another water-hole, taking care, as they went, to send up smoke signals to tell the tribe where they were, and whom they had met.

The smoke language is not nearly so perfect as the sign language, but still there are signals for most of the people and places in the country. Our boys could generally tell us where the stockmen were camped each night, and if they had met any white travellers.

'Blackfellow smoke bin talk, boy bin send him,' Jimmy said once when I asked him how he knew. The stockmen's boys had evidently sent him a telegraphic smoke message. As Bett-Bett wandered about the bush there was no danger that she would lose herself. A white child cannot possibly lose itself in its nursery and neither could Bett-Bett in hers, even though it stretched for about a hundred miles.

She talked a lot about the bush this night, and told me that Debbil-debbils are very frightened of dogs, and that if every one is very quiet the Debbil-debbils cannot find them. When she hears Debbil-debbils about, she never speaks and then they go away. Sue of course could frighten them off; but as she is a very little dog, and Debbil-debbils are very big and strong, it is just as well to take no risks. I believe that if Debbil-debbils did ever carry Sue off, Bett-Bett would insist on going too, for life without her would not be worth living.

Before I sent Bett-Bett to bed, I asked her if she would like to come a 'walk-about' on horseback next time we went.

'My word, Missus!' she cried, springing to her feet, and then added politely—

'Dank you please, Missus!' and then called Sue to come and dream of the glories of such a walk-about. Next morning I heard shrieks of laughter and shouts of—

'Go and lay 'em egg, silly fellow you.'

I went to see what it was all about, and found Bett-Bett and the lubras doubled up with laughter at old 'Broody,' who seemed to be turning double somersaults and Catherine wheels across the grass patch.

Bett-Bett had been right, and the crocodile's egg had hatched. The little curled-up creature had suddenly unwound itself, and splintering the shell into fragments had headed straight for the water.

Poor old Broody! we saw nothing of her for days, but when next we heard her, she was announcing to all the world that she had taken Bett-Bett's advice and had 'gone and laid an egg.'

Bett-Bett appeared, grinning wisely, and said—

'That one hen no more broody now, Missus.'

I said that she might have the egg for herself, so she took it and roasted it in the fire. Before laying it on the hot ashes I noticed that she chipped a ring right round it with her finger nails, taking great care not to pierce the skin underneath the shell.

'What name likee that, Bett-Bett?' I asked.

Carefully covering it up with ashes, she answered, 'Spose me no more break him, him break meself all about.'

'Topsy was sitting among the women-folk'

9

The Coronation 'Playabout'

We were camped at the Bitter Springs on the Roper River, about fifteen miles from home, and had just shut up a big mob of cattle in the yards.

We had been 'out bush' for a couple of weeks, riding from camp to camp, and mustering as we went. Bett-Bett was with us for her promised treat, and, as the head stockman said, was having 'a wild and woolly time.' Perched straddle-legs on an old stock-horse, with the stirrup-irons wedged firmly between her little bare toes, she had had many a wild gallop after the cattle; and that, and everything else, was better than her wildest dreams of camping out.

As we rode from the yards to our camp, one of the men said:

'Isn't this June? because, if it is, I reckon King Edward will be just about crowned.'

We all agreed it was June right enough, but nobody seemed sure of the date; we couldn't even decide what day of the week it was. We had been 'out bush' so long that we had got hopelessly mixed.

'Well,' said the Maluka, 'we're within a week of it, and that's near enough for the Never-Never; so we'll have a 'play-about' to celebrate it. Whoop! Hallo there, boys!' he called; 'come and have a bigfellow play-about.' Then remembering that some bush blacks were camped at the river, he added, 'Call up your pals, and I'll shoot you a bullock for yourselves.'

With yells and screechings they obeyed, and were answered back by louder yells, as their bush friends— about twenty men, women and children—came screaming through the trees to accept the invitation.

Some hobbled the horses, some collected firewood, others dug a big, wide, shallow hole, and lit an enormous fire in it; lubras and piccaninnies ran to hunt for stones, which were to be made red hot in the fire; and everybody scampered and scuffled about, getting in each other's way, laughing and shrieking, as they played practical jokes on one another. When they heard the shot that killed the bullock, they rushed off in a wild stampede to the stockyard.

In about ten minutes a ghastly procession came in sight, for the bullock had simply been hacked in pieces, skin and all; and every one, down to the tiniest piccaninny, was carrying a red, horrible-looking joint of meat.

Billy Muck, who was to be King himself some day, had the bullock's head, and was amusing himself and everybody else by bucking and charging around, digging the horns into any one he could catch. Bett-Bett had the tail, and was swishing about with it among the lubras and piccaninnies, greatly to their delight. In fact, the future King and Queen were quite the life of the party. As the procession dodged and jumped about, it reminded me of a troop of clowns at a circus.

When it reached the fire, the meat was thrown on the ground, and while the dogs were helping themselves to the tit-bits, the ashes and stones were scraped out, and then the oven was ready for the joints.

A layer of hot stones was first thrown in, then some joints of meat, then more stones and more meat, layer after layer, till the hole was full and heaped up; on top of this were poured a few quarts of water, on top again was piled earth, and on top of everything else a great big fire was lit.

Then we went to our own camp to supper, and the blacks, making little fires every here and there, grilled small pieces of meat, to take the edge off their appetites; for it would be quite two hours before the joints were ready to eat.

As they sat, singing their strange, weird songs, the head stockman said it was a pity that we had no fireworks; but as his Majesty would not let his mail-man carry them, it was his Majesty's own fault, not ours.

'What about a Poolooloomee Show?' suggested the Maluka.

Tonald slept peacefully in his pretty little cradle (*top*).
Murraweedbee at home.

'Poolooloomees, boys!' we shouted, and every blackfellow sprang to his feet with a yell. Snatching tomahawks, knives and hatchets, they rushed to the tall, white gum trees, and peeled off great sheets of bark, for they dearly loved a 'Poolooloomee Play-about.'

They dragged the bark to the fire, and sitting down, cut it into thick strips, which were trimmed and shaped till they looked like small-sized tennis racquets, or rather long-handled battledores. As these were cut, the lubras put the broad ends into the fires, leaving the handles sticking safely out. They did not blaze, for the bark was too full of sap, but they gradually changed colour till they were beautiful glowing rings of fire.

Of course, as soon as half-a-dozen were ready to send off, the blacks wanted to fire them, and the Maluka had hard work to make them wait till everybody was well supplied with Poolooloomees. He managed it somehow, and it was well worth the trouble, for we had a magnificent display of fireworks.

When about two hundred of these little racquets were cut and glowing, each blackfellow drove a strong, straight rod into the ground, and holding one Poolooloomee high in his right hand, and a bundle of others in his left, stood looking at the Maluka, waiting for a signal.

'Let her go, Gallagher!' he shouted, and instantly the air was full of yells, and blazing, twirling, curling hoops of fire—the Poolooloomee Show had begun.

At the word of command, every man had brought his right arm down with a peculiar short, sharp swing, and striking the Poolooloomee handles hard against the firm upright rods, had broken off the fiery circles, and sent them whirling and twisting and soaring high up into the air. Quick as lightning, the handles were dropped, other Poolooloomees taken from the left hand, struck off, and sent circling and sailing after the first flight, to be followed again and again by others.

It was marvellously weird and beautiful. Up went the strange fireworks, shooting like rockets through the trees, to join the brilliant cloud of Poolooloomees that were floating away into the glorious tropical night. Backwards and forwards among the fires raced the lubras looking like flitting black shadows, as they carried fresh supplies of fireworks to the men, letting no one's left hand get quite empty. The men themselves, standing full in the light of the fires, looked like shining black giants, as they worked and yelled and hallooed at their posts, surprised both at themselves and their display; and we whites sat still in wonder, amazed and admiring, sorry only that so few of the civilized world were there to see it all.

Poolooloomees are really a Daly Water's Play-about, but our Roper blacks had learnt it from them, and some had learnt it very well.

As the last few Poolooloomees glided out of sight, we gave a 'Hip, hip, hooray!' and a 'Tiger' for King Edward VII, and then amused ourselves by trying to fire some more.

Most of our attempts were dismal failures; the Poolooloomees doing exactly what they ought not to do. All I fired tried to bury themselves in the ground, and the head stockman's spent most of their time hitting the nearest tree, and burning everybody within reach with a shower of sparks.

Altogether we had a merry time, and the blacks cut away at bark for us, and screamed with delight at our failures; and when one of the Maluka's rockets bounced from a tree, and dived into the head stockman's much-cherished grass-bed, their joy knew no bounds. But when it blazed up, they rushed to the rescue and beat the fire out, looking like so many black imps, as they danced among the flames.

After that they dug each other in the ribs with hot fire-sticks, and played most foolish and painful jokes till the bullock was cooked. When the earth and fire were at last scraped away, everybody helping themselves to huge junks, and began tearing at them like wild beasts, dog and master eating from the same joint. I called Bett-Bett then, and we went to our camp, leaving our guests to their feast; for this part of the entertainment was not very pretty.

Long after midnight they were still at it, singing and laughing and feasting. As I lay awake listening to them, I heard a peculiar scrunching going on inside Bett-Bett's mosquito net. I went over to see what it was, and found that she had crept back to the feast for her precious ox-tail, and that she and Sue were just finishing picking the bones.

Next morning the bullock had completely disappeared, and the

King's loyal subjects looked as though they would burst, if only pricked with a pin!

When we reached the homestead we found we had been a few days too soon with our demonstration; so on the proper day we called the blacks up, and gave them flour, and treacle, and 'chewbac,' for we had no bullock in the yards. Every one got an equal share, and Jimmy carried his supply in his little Union Jack apron, which was most loyal of him; the only unpleasant thing about it was, that when he took his apron off, he had nothing left in the way of clothes.

As the blacks turned to go to their camp, the men gave another 'Hip Hooray and a Tiger' for the King, and then fired a volley of revolver shots into the air as a royal salute. This was too much for our dusky friends; they thought we had suddenly gone mad, and dropping flour and treacle-tins in all directions, fled helter-skelter into the bush, even Bett-Bett and the piccaninnies joining in the general scamper.

We shouted to them to stop, and said we were only having a 'play-about'; but they did not wait to hear. We ran after them, but that only made matters worse. The only thing was to sit down and wait. When all was quiet, I lifted up my voice to the high sing-song pitch that the lubras had taught me would carry well, and I called Bett-Bett.

Away in the distance a thin little squeak answered. Then I called again and again, and at last she screwed up enough courage to come back. We sent her after the others, to tell them we were only in fun, and to say they had better come and collect their tucker.

For about five minutes we heard her shrill little voice piping through the forest, and then Billy Muck turned up, giggling nervously. Soon after him came the station 'Boys,' trying hard to look at ease, and pretending they had only run for fun. But it was nearly half-an-hour before everybody decided that it was really safe.

The last man in got teased unmercifully because he had been frightened of the Missus and the Boss—the good 'Maluka' who was every blackfellow's friend— and I thought it was very like 'the pot calling the kettle black,' seeing how they had run themselves.

We told them that we had shouted and fired, because that is the way that white men always have a Play-about Corrobboree. They seemed able to see some sense in that idea, and were soon shouting with laughter at the way they had run, as though it were the best joke in the world.

Bett-Bett put on great airs because she had come back first, and strutted about with her nose in the air, saying; 'Me no more frightened fellow longa Missus; me all day savey Boss play-about. Me no more run long way,' and so on, and so on.

As nobody had waited to see, nobody could contradict her, and she had it all her own way, and 'came out on top,' as the men said.

After a while everything was gathered up again, and new pipes were given out all round to make up for the fright, and very soon some most indigestible-looking dampers were cooked and eaten, and every one was happy and contented.

The King had Coronation demonstrations all over his empire, and at many of them a whole ox may have been roasted in the good old English way; but I doubt if he had a stranger or a merrier one than ours, in the very heart of the Never-Never Land.

Some weeks afterwards we heard of the King's illness, and of the postponing of the Coronation, and knew that after all we had missed the real Coronation Day, but we had paid our homage to our King, and we were satisfied.

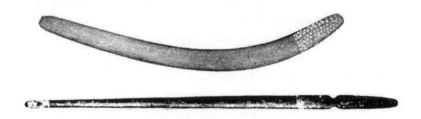

Boomerang and Throwing-stick.

10

'Looking-Out Lily-Root'

Bett-Bett and I very often went down to the billabong for an early morning 'bogey,' and she and the lubras were always greatly amused at my bathing-gown. They called it 'that one bogey dress,' and said it was 'silly fellow.'

My swimming also amused them. They saw something very comical and unnatural in my movements, and I often caught them imitating me. They seemed to expect me to sink every moment, and never went very far from me in case of accidents.

One morning we swam right across the billabong to the 'nuzzer side,' as Bett-Bett called it, and there I noticed a man's tracks on the bank, and asked whose they were; for of course I did not recognize them. To my surprise the lubras burst into shrieks of laughter.

'Him Maluka!' they shouted in delight; 'him track belonga Maluka; him bin bogey last night.' Then Bett-Bett screamed to the lubras on the opposite bank—

'Missus no more savey track belonga Boss.'

It was the best joke they had ever heard—a woman who did not know her own husband's tracks! I felt very small indeed, and as soon as possible went back to the house and breakfast.

We were going to have fowls for dinner, which always meant great fun for the blacks. The whole camp generally appeared with sticks and stones, and when the cook had pointed out which fowls were to be caught, almost exciting chase took place. Off the birds at the first alarm, followed by a shrieking, yelling crowd, flying over and under everything, and dodging round corners, till they were at last run down. I tried often to prevent it, but no matter how carefully the birds were shut up over night, they always managed to get out. The blacks enjoyed the chase so thoroughly that I suspect the fowls were assisted in their escape. Bett-Bett and Sue were of course in the worst of it this day, and by some mishap a stone, meant for one of the fowls, struck Sue on the front legs. She ran yelping and limping to Bett-Bett, and then I heard shrieks of—

'Missus! Missus! Sue bin break him arm. Stone bin kill him,' and they both appeared at the door. I took the poor little dog, and found it was only too true; one of her arms—as the blacks insist on calling the front legs—was hanging limp and broken. I bound it up as well as I could, and Bett-Bett cried piteously because I hurt the little creature.

When everything was made quite comfortable, she took Sue and sat nursing and crooning over her all the morning.

In the afternoon the Maluka and I were starting out for a ride, when Bett-Bett appeared with the lubras.

They were going to travel 'per boot' or on foot. Slung across Bett-Bett's back was a most ingenious sack-like affair, and from it peeped Sue's comical little face; for Bett-Bett could not bear either to leave her at home, or to see her limping about.

We were only going about three miles, and as it was too rough and too hot to travel quickly, the lubras kept up with us easily. I noticed that Murraweedbee was with them, and was still dragging her branch. I asked her if she had seen anything of her husband, and she said— 'You eye. Him Monkey longa Willeroo.'

Then I was told that Murraweedbee was really our Big Jack's lubra, but that Monkey had carried her off, the day that we had found Bett-Bett. Monkey had been very cruel to her, and so she had watched her chance and run back to Jack. It was a most interesting love-story, and the exciting part was that Monkey was supposed to be somewhere rather near. Suspicious tracks had been seen. When we arrived at the Warlock Ponds —our destination— we found that some of the homestead blacks were there—all lubras, gathering lily-roots for their husbands' supper.

When lubras go 'looking out lily-root,' as they call it, they take with them tiny little wooden canoes, about two feet long, called coolamuns. They leave these floating about on the top of the water, while they themselves drop down to the bottom for the bulbs. As soon as their hands are full, they come up again, and putting the roots into the little vessels, disappear for more.

The Warlocks are always very beautiful ponds, all fringed round with pandanus palms, and dotted everywhere with magnificent purple waterlilies, but this day they looked like a peep into fairyland. As I sat on my horse looking at it, I thought I had never seen anything prettier than the little, dainty, rocking canoes, sailing among the blossoms, as the bobbing, curly, black heads of the lubras appeared and disappeared.

When the lubras saw us, they swam over, pushing the coolamuns before them, and as they came nearer I saw that in two of them were wee black piccaninnies; for a coolamun may be either a cradle or a tucker basket.

There is no fear of their upsetting, for they are beautifully balanced, and even on land are very hard to overturn; besides, if the baby did scramble out, it would not matter, for most likely it would only swim about till its mother came up. I think if I were a baby, I would like to lie in my little canoe, as it rocked and danced among the lilies.

Suddenly Bett-Bett gave the alarm, and the air was filled with ear-splitting shrieks and yells, as every one pointed to a nigger's tracks, and said they were a Willeroo's, and that he was running quickly. Murraweedbee pushed forward to see, and then giving a yell of 'Monkey!' started for the homestead like an arrow from a bow, the branch bobbing and dancing and leaping behind her.

It looked as though an explosion of dynamite had taken place, for every one, seizing the nearest coolamun or tucker basket, ran helter-skelter after her. Only Bett-Bett and a poor blind lubra, 'Lose-'em Eye,' as she was called, stayed behind. Bett-Bett preferred white folk and revolvers when Willeroos were about; perhaps she was also thinking of poor Sue's foot.

My word. Missus! You cheeky fellow alright,' said Charlie...'

'South of the Roper River dead men are always put away in the
brances for a long time before burial.'

We started for home with Bett-Bett and Lose-'em Eye between the horses for safety. At the creek a valiant army met us, setting out to overtake and conquer Monkey. It was headed by old Jimmy, who had borrowed an old rusty revolver, and was full of courage to the finger-tips. He also had old Nellie in tow, to show where the tracks had been seen.

About sundown the valiant army returned, still thirsting for Monkey's blood; for although they followed him a long way, his tracks were always new, and running westward. He evidently was doing a quick passage home.

After much excitement we were of course told most awful stories of Willeroos, particularly of Monkey, and Murraweedbee was the heroine of the hour.

Bett-Bett said that once she had been caught by them with some lubras and piccaninnies, and all the lubras said they remembered it well. It was a fearful tale, and a fearful experience. They were made to travel very quickly because of pursuit, and at supper time there was no tucker, so the Willeroos killed some of the piccaninnies and ate them, and then went to sleep. Fortunately in the morning some stockmen, who had been following the tracks, rode into the camp, and the Willeroos took to their heels, and that time the Roper River lubras escaped, Bett-Bett among them.

I asked her how it had happened that she had not been killed and eaten, and she answered with a chuckle—

'Me too muchee all day bone fellow'—she had evidently not been worth eating, when fatter piccaninnies were about! 'Me all day bone fellow,' she repeated, holding out a thin little arm. She seemed to think she had been very clever in being thin, and she certainly had been fortunate!

Poor little mite! she had seen some fearful doings in her short life.

When I asked her if she had eaten any of these piccaninnies, she said that the blackfellows had not left any for her. 'Blackfellow bin finissem, Missus,' was all she said, and I don't believe she would have refused to have eaten her share.

She lay for a while looking up at the sky, and then changed the conversation by saying—

'Missus, I think big-fellow blackfellow close up finissem, that one moon.'

'What?' I said, looking at the thin little strip of new moon.

'I think big-fellow blackfellow close up finissem, that one moon,' she repeated, jerking her voice, as she jerked her finger, towards it,

'Whatever are you talking about, Bett-Bett?' I asked.

She sat up and looked at me in surprise, and asked what did happen to the moon if a 'big-fellow, big-fellow blackfellow'—a giant, I suppose—didn't cut it up to make the stars? All the lubras sat up too, and agreed with her, saying, 'Straightfellow, Missus.' Even Sue joined in the conversation, but perhaps that was because some one had planted an enthusiastic elbow on her tail.

'Me plenty savey,' said Bett-Bett, lying down again. Then she told me that away out east there is a beautiful country, where a big tribe of moons live, hundreds of them. They are very silly creatures, and will wander about in the sky alone—you never see two moons at once, you know! Whenever a new moon wanders into the west—she called a full moon a new one—a great big giant who lives there, catches it and snips big pieces off and makes stars with them. Some of the moons get away before he can cut them all up, but this poor moon had been 'close up finissem,' first thing.

'Spose me moon,' said Bett-Bett, 'me stay in my country; me no more silly fellow.'

The suns live out east too, and are a very powerful tribe of 'cheeky fellows.' Every day one of them goes straight across the sky, and nobody knows what happens to him. At least no lubra knows. Of course the wise men know everything.

I suggested that perhaps the sun went back at night, but the lubras said if he did everybody would see him, and so, I supposed, they would.

Stars are very frightened of the sun. They say he is a 'cheeky fellow,' and will 'round them up,' if he finds them in the sky; so they hide all day, and towards night send two or three of the bravest of them to peep out, and see if he is really gone.

'Look, Missus,' said Bett-Bett, pointing up at the sky. 'Littlefellow star come on now. Him look this way. Him look that way. Him talk which way sun sit down,' and it seemed, as I watched, as if they really were peeping cautiously about. Suddenly raising her voice to its very highest and shrillest pitch, she called— 'Sun bin go away alright.'

After she had called, a great number of stars came quickly one after the other, and she got very excited about it.

'Him bin hear me, Missus,' she cried. 'Straightfellow! Him bin hear me.'

After a long silence Bett-Bett said—'Might it God bin make star longa you country, Missus?'

I only said, 'You eye, God bin make my star,' Long ago I had given up trying to make them understand anything, excepting that God was a great good Spirit, who was not afraid of the fiercest of Debbil-debbils, and would chase them away from any one if they would ask Him. I had made them understand that much, and after many months they were beginning to believe it. In my first experiences with them I had told them that God had made all things; and of course they had wanted to know how He made them, and what He had made them of. They assured me He had not made anything in the blackfellow's country. The wise men had an explanation of how everything there had been made, but I knew nothing of God's mysterious ways, and could explain nothing; so I decided to teach them first to believe in God Himself, and to let the other things alone.

Bett-Bett's thoughts were evidently on those early lessons, for soon she asked why God had not made any 'bush' in the white man's country. A country without a 'bush' was a constant puzzle to her. Old Goggle Eye had once gone a trip to a big town as 'boy' with a mob of cattle, and had come back with the astonishing news that in the white man's country there was no 'bush,' only tracks and humpies.

Goggle Eye had gone to Western Australia in a steamer with these cattle, but had walked home, because, he said, the steamer had 'Too muchee jump-up jump-up, too muchee jump-down jump-down; me all day barcoo' (sick).

Before Bett-Bett went to bed she once more repeated— 'Blackfellow bin make this one mob star, Missus.' Poor mite! she had no idea that her 'mob' and my 'mob' were the same 'mob.'

Rolly lingered behind every one, and asked if she might sleep under the verandah this night. Poor Rolly was often very ill, and then was very frightened of Debbil-debbils and liked to sleep near me. She said Debbil-debbils could not come near where I was, because 'Bigfellow God all day look out longa you, Missus.' So, you see that after all my trouble in teaching them, I had given them the idea that I was God's especial care.

It is very, very hard work to teach any blackfellow the truth of God's goodness and love. They have no god of any sort themselves, and they cannot imagine one.

After our Willeroo scare we did not wander 'out bush' at all, for two reasons. The fear of Monkey was upon us, and Sue's foot needed rest.

11

'Newfellow Piccaninny Boy'

One morning, a few weeks after our Willeroo scare, Bett-Bett came scampering up from the creek as fast as her thin little legs would carry her. 'Missus! Missus!' she shouted, 'Topsy bin catch newfellow piccaninny boy, Topsy bin catch newfellow piccaninny boy,' and she sank down in a little breathless heap beside me.

Fast on her heels came some of the camp lubras bringing me an invitation to the christening party.

'You eye,' they gasped, 'him bin catch him alright,' and then they told me that Topsy, Sambo's lubra, wanted me to come and see it, and christen it with a white man's name. 'Topsy bin talk, spose Missus come on, give piccaninny whitefellow name.'

Of course I went at once, taking a good supply of 'chewbac' and a big red handkerchief, for we did not have a christening every day. Besides, I was curious to see this baby, for I had not yet seen a very tiny piccaninny.

Sambo met us at the creek, grinning widely with delight. We gave the proud father a new pipe and some 'chewbac,' and he tried hard to grin a little wider in thanks, but found that even a blackfellow's grin has its limits. Topsy was sitting among the lubras, and looked round when she heard us approaching, On her knee was her eldest son 'Bittertwine,' a chubby little rascal about two years old. Beside her lay a coolamun, nearly filled with fresh green leaves and grass. As I came nearer she lifted up some of the leaves and showed me the tiniest, tiniest atom of a baby lying sound asleep; cool, and safe from flies, in its pretty leafy cradle.

I stood for some minutes, too astonished to speak, for instead of the shiny jet-black piccaninny I had expected, I found one just about the colour of honey.

'What name, Topsy?' I asked at last. 'Him close up whitefellow, I think.'

'No more, Missus,' she answered, touching the little sleeping baby lovingly. 'Him blackfellow alright. Look, Missus, him blackfellow alright,' she added, showing me one thin jet-black line running right round the mouth and others round the eyes and nails.

Then the lubras all joined in, and explained that a little black baby when it is first born, is always of a very light golden brown but with thin black lines, just as this baby had. They said that steadily and surely these lines would widen and spread till in a few days he would be like all other shiny black piccaninnies.

'All day likee that, Missus,' they assured me in chorus, so I put a handful of tobacco in the baby's cradle, and spread a big red handkerchief on top. I said he was a man baby and Mr. Thunder Debbil-debbil would be delighted to see he had a nice red handkerchief. The lubras laughed merrily at this, and the old men smiled on the Missus with approval.

Then Topsy asked for a 'whitefellow name' for her baby, and I said he should be called 'Donald.'

'Tonald!' cried Topsy. 'Tonald! Him good-fellow name, that one.'

Every one repeated 'Tonald' after her, and then called to each other. 'Missus bin talk Tonald,' and the whole camp agreed it was a 'goodfellow name alright.' For some reason, best known to themselves, the name pleased them.

Topsy said that her baby had a kangaroo's spirit, and Jimmy was very pleased and important about it.

You see, Jimmy was head man of the Kangaroo-spirit family, and it would be his duty to see that 'Tonald' was properly brought up, for he must be taught all the laws of his Totem, as well as how to throw his boomerang and use his throwing-stick. Jimmy was a sort of godfather to him, and Tonald would have to obey him even more than his own father and mother.

'By and by me make him grow, Missus,' said Jimmy, meaning

that he would perform some very important ceremony to make the Debbil-debbils keep away so that Tonald could grow into a strong wise blackfellow. It was Jimmy's duty to do this, and a blackfellow always does his duty to his tribe.

After the christening I passed round some 'chewbac' and every one's pipe was filled, and Tonald's health was smoked. Every now and then an old blackfellow would nod his head and chuckle.

'Tonald! Him goodfellow name that one.'

But Donald slept peacefully on, and Bittertwine sat on his mother's knee, looking from me to the piccaninny, with big wondering eyes. Every little while he took his mother's pipe out of her mouth, and put it in his own for a few sucks—smoking Donald's health, I suppose.

Bittertwine was a wild little black boy or 'myall,' and terrified of white men, but I don't think it was the white man's fault. I fancy his mother used to tell him that the white man would catch him if he were naughty. Just as some white mothers say 'the black man' will catch *their* piccaninnies.

When we called on 'Tonald' next morning I found that Sambo was wearing his handkerchief and that his friends had smoked his tobacco.

Topsy was very proud of her piccaninny. 'Look, Missus,' she said. 'Him close up blackfellow now.' So he was, and a day or two afterwards he was black all over, all excepting the palms of his hands and the soles of his feet. These would be a pale grey all his life.

There was a visitor in the camp, quite a civilized blackfellow called Charlie, who was a great authority on christenings, for he had once been in a Catholic Mission School. He told us that when a white piccaninny got a name that 'whitefellow chuck em water longa piccaninny.' He had been christened himself once, and water had been 'chucked' on him, and he seemed to think he knew all about it. The priests used to tell a great joke about him. Charlie had been taught that he must not eat meat on a Friday, but one Friday he was found with a piece of beef.

'Charlie,' said the priest sternly, 'you are eating meat.'

'No more,' said Charlie, seriously. 'This one fish alright.'

The priest then said it was very wicked to say what was not true, but Charlie insisted that his beef *was* fish.

'Yes,' he said, arguing it out. 'This one fish alright,' and then he told the priest that they had christened him with water, and called him Charlie, so he had christened his beef with water and called it fish.
'You bin chuck 'em water longa me, you bin call me Charlie. Alright *me* bin chuck 'em water longa beef, *me* bin call *fish*,' and he quietly went on eating his fish.

Charlie came up to the house a few days after the christening, and very rudely demanded a 'big mob of chewbac.'

I felt very angry with him for coming to me like this when he knew I was alone, so I said as quietly as I could—

'Very well, I'll give you a big mob of something, Charlie,' and before he quite knew what had happened he was looking at my revolver, as I pointed it straight at him.

Poor Charlie, he could hardly be seen for the dust he made, in his hurry to get out of revolver range. That was the first and last time I had to take my revolver to a blackfellow, but Charlie was supposed to be civilized, you see. You cannot change a blackfellow into a white man, if you try; you only make a bad cunning sly old blackfellow. I don't mean you can't make a blackfellow into a better blackfellow. I know that can be done, if he is kept a blackfellow, true to his blackfellow instincts.

After this I expected that Charlie would keep out of my way, but he didn't; he now seemed to consider himself a very special friend of mine.

'My word, Missus! you cheeky fellow alright,' he said next morning, when I went down to the camp, and he sat in front of a little circle of blackfellows, looking up at me in admiration.

'My word!' echoed the old fellows, for Charlie had told his story, and my old friends, being blackfellows, were full of reverence for any one who was a 'cheeky fellow.'

As we sat talking, Charlie told us that God made everything a white man has—trains and watches and horses, and that He showed him how to know miles. A blackfellow can see nothing to mark a mile, and wonders how the white man can. 'Me plenty savey,' said Charlie, 'me savey count all about,' and he began to count his fingers. He kept getting mixed and that meant beginning at his thumb again, and it was not till after many struggles that he managed to count to five.

'My word!' everybody said, and Charlie swelled with pride. You see a blackfellow only counts up to two. His arithmetic is very simple, just —One, Two, Little Mob, Big Mob, so it was no wonder we were all amazed at Charlie.

He then told us in confidence that a little Debbil-debbil 'sat down' inside the telegraph wire, and ran messages 'quickfellow,' from one telegraph station to another. 'Me savey,' he said wisely; 'me bin hear him talk-talk longa Daly Waters.' Then, looking gravely round, he added: 'Him bite alright, that one little fellow Debbil-debbil.'

I laughed at this, and the old men giggled nervously, for we all knew that he had done what nearly every Aboriginal has done—he had climbed up a telegraph pole to break off a piece of wire for a spear, and had found out that the Debbil-debbil could bite when he got an electric shock! He said it didn't bite the white man because he was its master. The very fiercest dog never bites his master, you know!

Charlie knew all about that telegraph line. It was really a fence to keep the kangaroos in. That was why it was so high—too high for them to jump over. Unfortunately, the white man used up all the wire he had for the two top rails, and couldn't finish it. When the little Debbil-debbil 'jumped in,' he made him run messages 'quickfellow' for him.

'My word, whitefellow plenty savey,' said Jimmy.

Billy Muck agreed with him, but said he was a 'big-fellow fool' when he rounded up a big mob of cattle, and worked hard day and night only to brand them and let them go again. If Billy owned cattle he would kill them all and invite his friends to the feast. Somehow as I sat looking at the generous, honest, simple, unspoiled, blackfellow—absolutely free from vice or care—I felt that perhaps he was right, and the white man is a 'bigfellow fool,' after all.

Charlie didn't like Billy's getting so much attention, and offered to count his toes, but I was tired of Charlie and his civilized ways, so called Bett-Bett and went home.

Bett-Bett was fascinated with Tonald and asked all sorts of questions about white piccaninnies. Were they born white? Did they wear clothes? and so on.

To amuse her, I made a rag doll, and painted a face on it, and dressed it like a baby. She looked at it for a long while, feeling it carefully all over, then she said with a chuckle—

'Him gammon piccaninny I think, Missus!'

All the first day she carried it in her arms, and Charlie told great tales of 'gammon piccaninnies' that broke if they fell down.

The next day she said that 'gammon piccaninnies' were 'silly fellow.'

The day after that, Sue and the station pups had a tug-of-war with it, and the last we saw of it was when Sue was 'going bush' with it in her mouth, and the pups in full chase after her.

Bett-Bett took no notice of the fate of her 'gammon piccaninny.' She had found something much more interesting—a nest of little kittens under the raised floor of the bath-room—and for several days we saw very little of her, except the soles of her feet, as they stuck out from under the bath-room floor.

When the kittens were big enough, I sent Billy Muck with one of them to my next-door neighbour. With a bottle of milk and a saucer under one arm, and the kitten under the other, he started for his hundred-mile walk as cheerfully as though he were just going round the corner, and in two days reached the Katherine, his journey's end.

On his return I asked him why he had hurried so.

'Milk close up finissem,' was all he said.

Good kind old Billy Muck! He wouldn't let even a kitten suffer from hunger or thirst, if he could help it.

1 2

Goggle Eye sung 'Deadfellow'

'Missus!' a thin, cracked old voice whispered close to me as I sat sewing one evening. I looked up to see an old, old grey-haired black-fellow standing beside me.

'What name?' I said, feeling rather startled, and then something in his face made me look more closely at him, and I saw that it was Goggle Eye; but oh, such a worn old scarecrow! There was hardly a trace of the merry, laughing rogue, who had gone off, a few weeks before, with his bag of sugar tied round his neck. 'Poor old Goggle Eye!' I said, 'whatever has happened?' 'Blackfellow bin sing me deadfellow longa bush,' he croaked in a hoarse whisper. 'Flour-bag bin come on quickfellow longa me cobra,' he added, pointing to his grey old head, with its thickly-sprinkled 'flour-bag,' as he called the white hairs. I knew what this singing meant. He had been cursed —as completely as the little thieving 'Jackdaw of Rheims'—by the magic men of the tribe. They had bewitched him by singing magic, and pointing death-bones at him, and he would die. Nothing that I could do would save him.

He looked so weak and worn that I gave him some brandy, and he laydown under the verandah. As he lay there, he told me that Tommy Dod, a blackfellow, had carried him thirty miles on his back to bring him in to me and the homestead. Tommy Dod was his younger blood-brother, and it was his duty to help the poor old fellow.

Supposing that he was going to make Goggle Eye die by magic, this is what he would sing: —

Kill Goggle Eye, kill Goggle Eye, make him deadfellow; Pull away his fat, make him bone fellow; Shut him up throat, shut him up throat; Break him out heart, break him out heart; Kill him deadfellow, kill him deadfellow; Spose him eat fish, poison him with it; Spose him eat bird, poison him with it.

And he would keep on singing, till he had sung or cursed everything he could think of; but he would not try to 'sing water,' for nobody can do that.

Any one can 'sing magic,' even lubras, but of course the wise old magic men do it best. It never fails with them, particularly if they 'sing' and point one of the 'Special Death-bones,' or 'Sacred Stones' of the tribe. Generally a blackfellow goes away quite by himself when he is 'singing magic,' but very occasionally a few men join together, as they did in the case of Goggle Eye.

When enough magic has been 'sung' into the bone, it is taken away to the camp, and very secretly pointed at the unconscious victim. The magic spirit of the bone runs into the man who is pointed at, and gradually kills him.

Everything must be done very secretly, for if the man's relatives had any idea who had done the bone-pointing, they would go and 'sing' him in revenge. You must be particularly careful that there are no Willy-Waggle-tails or 'Jenning-gherries' about, for these little mischief-makers would go and tell the cockatoos, who in their turn would make a dream about it, and carry it to the bewitched man when he was asleep, to let him know who had 'sung' him.

Cockatoos make all the dreams, and carry them to the sleepers in the night. If you are lying awake, you may often hear them moving in the dark, for they are very restless birds. The best time to point bones is at night, for then all 'Jenning-gherries' are asleep.

Of course the man who has been 'sung' must be told somehow, or he will not get a fright and die. There are many ways of managing this; one very good way is to put the bone where he will be sure to find it, in his dilly-bag, or near his fire, or through the handle of his spear. There are many ways of telling him, without letting him know who has 'sung' him; but the man who leaves the bone about must, of course, be very careful to his own tracks.

Have you ever heard of faith-healing? well, dying from bone-pointing is faith-dying! Goggle Eye, after he had found the bones lying about, knew exactly what was going to happen to him—and of course it did. His throat got very sore, and he grew so thin and weak that he could barely stand.

A man can be cured by magic men charming the 'bone' away again; but Goggle Eye was old, and what was worse, he was getting very cross, and too fond of ordering people about, so the blackfellows thought that it would be the best plan not to cure him, and a few more sneaked away into the bush and 'sang' some more 'bones' and pointed them at him, to make quite sure about his dying.

It was fearfully cruel. Poor old Goggle Eye suffered so dreadfully, and the only friend he had—excepting the Missus—was Tommy Dod! Nobody else would do anything for him, because they were afraid of the curse coming to them. It couldn't touch Tommy, because he was his blood-brother, and had to do all he could to help.

Old Jimmy and Billy Muck said they would like to help, but that if they made Goggle Eye's fire for him, their own would never burn again. Nobody could even carry his food to him. To make matters worse, Tommy Dod had to go 'bush' on some private business—perhaps he was singing some of his own enemies dead—and then I had to do everything myself.

Day after day I took his food to him, and made his fire, but I soon saw that it was too late. He ate anything that I brought him, and ordered me about generally, and growled at me for not putting enough sugar in his tea— he didn't want sugar in his tea, what he preferred was a little tea in his sugar!

Sometimes a glimpse of the merry old rogue would peep out from the gaunt old skeleton. One day I was on my hands and knees at his fire, blowing hard at it.

'My word, Missus,' he laughed merrily, 'you close up blow him all away,' and he showed me the proper way to blow, and chuckled to himself at my clumsy attempts; for a blackfellow can make a fire better than any one else.

It sounds very grand being a Lady-in-waiting to a King, but it really was very smelly and disagreeable. His humpy was in fact only a sheet of bark leaning against a fallen tree, and I had to crawl about on my hands and knees, and everything was dreadfully close and stuffy. But I had plenty of Eue de Cologne, and used it freely. One day when Bett-Bett smelt it, as I was sprinkling it over my dress, she screwed up her little black nose, and after half-a-dozen very audible sniffs, said—

'My word, Missus! That one goodfellow stink all right!'

I said I was glad she liked it, and as Goggle Eye also remarked on it, I always used plenty of this 'good-fellow stink' before I visited him.

At last Tommy Dod came back, and I had not so much to do. One evening, when I went up with some arrowroot, all the blacks in the camp were sitting round in a circle, looking at Goggle Eye. They had taken away the sheet of bark, so as to see him better, and were talking about him, and wondering when he would die, and if Debbil-debbils would take him away.

'I think him die to-night, Missus,' said Billy Muck cheerfully as I came up. 'I think him die fowl sing out.'

Goggle Eye gave a little glad cry when he saw me. 'Missus,' he called weakly, and I went to him and gave him a little brandy and arrowroot.

'Be quiet!' I said angrily, as the old men began talking about him again. They looked surprised, but obeyed, wondering, I think, why I objected to such an interesting topic of conversation.

Soon the poor old fellow asked me if I would tell my 'Big-Fellow God' to chase away the Debbil-debbils. I was very touched, and did exactly as he wished, in queer pidgin English. Then Goggle Eye was happy and contented, and the strange prayer was answered, for he was no longer afraid of his fearsome Debbil-debbils.

Soon after supper he fell asleep, and I left him, and never saw my strange old friend again. Billy Muck was right, and at 'fowl sing out' or cock-crow, Ebimel Wooloomool, King of Dullinarrinarr, died, and with him died many strange, weird old legends, and a good big slice of the history of the Blacks of the Never-Never.

Billy Muck, the Rainmaker, was now King, and I suppose that Bett-Bett was Queen Consort. But the tribe will never be afraid of the new King, for he is neither cute nor clever, and I don't think the wise men will take much notice of him. He is head man, of course, and knows all his Corroborees, but he is only a kind, simple-hearted old blackfellow, and will never be the absolute monarch that Goggle Eye was.

They buried the poor old King in a very shallow grave, just where he had died. They laid his spears, and his pipe, and all that belonged to him on the top of his grave, covering them over with a sheet of paper-bark, which was kept in place with a few large stones. After that they built his bark humpy over him again, and then went away, leaving him all alone in the deserted camp; for a camp is always deserted after a death. Their new camp was two or three hundred yards away, and never again would any one willingly enter the old one.

South of the Roper River dead men are always put away in the branches of a tree for a long time before burial, but I never heard of this being done at the Roper. I know Goggle Eye was buried at once, and there was a big 'cry-cry' in the camp. Every one ran about and pretended to cut themselves with knives, but I noticed that it was nearly all pretence. I don't believe that any one of them cared as much as I did.

Next day Tommy Dod started on a journey to try and find out, by different magic signs, who had 'sung' his brother, so that he could 'sing' them in revenge. That was his duty, you know. As far as I could find out, somebody was always looking for somebody else, in order to 'sing' him. If Tommy found the murderer he would 'sing' him, and if the murderer died his relatives would all 'sing' Tommy, and then Tommy's relatives would 'sing' the murderer's relatives, and that is how it goes on, till the wonder is that anybody is left alive.

Nobody ever mentioned Goggle Eye's name again. It really didn't matter, but it was just as well not to do so, because if he heard his name he might think some one was calling him, and come to see.

When they needed to speak of him, they gave his name in the sign language. To do this, they crooked up all their fingers till their hand looked like a bird's claw, and then suddenly jerked it forward, and that meant—'Ebimel Wooloomool Neckberrie,' or 'Goggle Eye the Deadfellow!'

Bett-Bett's 'wonderful, lonelyPalace' *(top)*.
All Goggle Eye's possessions, which were buried with him.

13

Bett-Bett is 'Bush-hungry'

For some days Bett-Bett had wandered about in an aimless, listless way, doing nothing and saying nothing, but just looking 'out bush' with big dreamy eyes.

She did not know what had happened to her, but I, who had seen this many times in her people, knew.

She was homesick—'bush hungry'—hungry for her own ways, and her own people; for the bush talks, and the camps, and the long long wanderings from place to place, for the fear of Debbil-debbils, for anything that would make her a little bush girl once more, for anything —if only she could shake off the white man for a little while, and do nothing but live.

We whites sometimes grow very weary and 'bush hungry' when we are taken away to the towns, but we can never even guess at the pain of a blackfellow's longing for his own people, and his beloved 'bush.'

Poor little Bett-Bett! as I watched her I knew that sooner or later I must let her go, for there was no other cure for her. If I tried to keep her, she would only run away or be ill.

At last she came to me saying—

'Missus! me sick-fellow, I think,' and sat down at my feet.

I talked to her quietly for a little while about her people, and their long walk-abouts; for the sooner she went, the quicker she would be cured.

All at once she knew what she needed.

'Missus,' she cried, springing to her feet, all life and energy again, 'Missus, me want walk-about. No more longa you, Missus, longa blackfellow.'

That was all—and I only asked—

'How long, Bett-Bett?'

'Me no more savey, Missus,' she answered, her eyes burning like stars. She could not tell. She only knew that she must stay till she was cured.

Next morning at 'sun up' she went. She took nothing with her but the little bag made from her 'Shimy Shirt' string, for in that were her most precious treasures. She stuffed all her clothes into her box, wearing only a gaily-striped handkerchief wound round her middle. Even that would soon be gone, for she was going to be just a little black girl for a while.

Sue didn't like the look of things at all. She sat down and whined miserably, trying to say that the homestead was quite good enough for her, as long as Bett-Bett was in it. Poor little Sue! It was really only her body that was so miserably ugly, for her comical little face was brimful of beautiful love and devotion for her little mistress.

I went as far as the camp with them, where Bett-Bett was to meet her friends. Then I stood and watched this tiny black Princess of the Never-Never, with her faithful speckled subject at her heels, fade away into her wonderful, lonely Palace. Once Sue sat down and whined, and Bett-Bett, looking round, saw me still watching her. She ran back, and without speaking, thrust a little pearl mussel-shell, one of her most treasured belongings, into my hand; then scampering after her friends, disappeared in the forest.

Then I walked back to the homestead, feeling strangely lonely, for I had grown accustomed to the little black shadow that was always chattering at my heels; but when I looked at the little pearl-shell, as it lay in my hand, I knew that in a little while Bett-Bett would need her 'Missus,' and come back bright and happy again.